On the beach at Vomo with Jeannette Stinson

Charles: Royal Adventurer

Don Coolican/Serge Lemoine

Pelham Books/Crown Publications

First published in Great Britain by
Pelham Books Ltd and Crown Publications Ltd
52 Bedford Square
London WC1B 3EF
1978

Copyright © 1978 Don Coolican and Serge Lemoine

ISBN 0 7207 1056 1

Printed by: Beric Press Ltd
                   Crawley
                   England

Originated by: Fleet Litho Ltd
                   Paul Street
                   London EC2

Typeset in: Times Roman 11/12pt.
        by: Premlux Reproductions Ltd
                   Old Bailey
                   London EC4

Bound by: Hunter Foulis Ltd
                   McDonald Road
                   Edinburgh
                   Scotland

Contents

Chapter 1
The White Charger

In an age when most princes are either living in
Mediterranean villas hoping to regain their throne,
or working as blue-blooded salesmen with noble
titles to get them by, or having their pictures taken
for gossip columns, Britain is a fortunate
kingdom. It has an heir to the throne who needs
only a white charger, golden sword and glistening
armour to complete the traditional picture of the
true prince.

To discover Prince Charles in adventurous,
sometimes dangerous situations, is as normal in
his life as finding one of the lesser of the princely
breeds relaxing at St Tropez. The latter is a role
that Prince Charles would enjoy to a certain
degree, but he is probably better described as one
of the last of the world's royal adventurers.

He wants to taste everything life can offer
and, with the privileges of his office to help him,
he fears nothing and ventures all.

The twenty-first Prince of Wales is on the
threshold of being a king. Until the day of his
coronation in Westminster Abbey he has set
himself one task above all others. He wishes to
learn at first hand as much as possible about the
people he will govern, and the kingdom he will
lead. He wants to experience as much of life as he
can in the years before the responsibilities of the
throne curb his adventurous spirit.

Queen Elizabeth the Queen Mother, once said
of her grandson: 'If there was anything left to
discover in the world, Charles would have been an
explorer.'

The Prince has said: 'I like to see if I can
challenge myself to do something that is
potentially hazardous, just to see if mentally I can
accept that challenge and carry it out. I like to try
all sorts of things because they appeal to me. I'm
one of those people who don't like sitting and
watching someone else doing something. I don't
like going to the races to watch horses thundering
up and down . . . I'd rather be riding the horses
myself.'

This dislike of just sitting and watching is
demonstrated to the limit when he is on official
tours abroad. To him the world appears as a huge
playground, with a variety of people to meet and

5

different ways of life to learn.

His special position in society makes it easier for him than for most other young men to try his hand at new and often daring experiences. A telephone call from the palace can usually fix most things, though many of his activities have been part of his training in the Royal Air Force and Royal Navy. He must be the envy of every schoolboy and a man admired by any young adult who has ever had Walter Mitty dreams.

Charles is a skilled frogman, has skippered ships, piloted helicopters, flown jet fighters, driven tanks, trained as a commando and made a parachute jump. He is also a top class horseman and polo player.

When not engaged in adventure pursuits, he carries out official royal duties, stays close to his family, keeps in touch with the worlds of art, literature, music, the theatre, politics and international affairs and still leads an active social life.

Charles also has great modesty, a wit which is appreciated by those around him, and a fine sensitivity. He admits that when he hears a piece of music by Berlioz 'I am so moved that I'm reduced to tears every time.'

During an official visit to Canada, Charles

was in the stark northern regions of his mother's realm. He visited Resolute Bay in the Northwest Territories in April 1975. He has been a sub-aqua swimmer for several years and could not resist joining a small band of divers who regularly plunge into the chillier parts of the Dominion.

His experience included training to escape from submarines, so he was no stranger to a frogman's suit. He has enjoyed the water from early childhood when he splashed around in the Buckingham Palace pool. Sinking beneath the Arctic ice, however, is only for the more daring marine brethren.

He went under the ice with a Canadian scientist, Dr Joe MacInnes of Undersea Research Limited, who has his headquarters over a narrow hole in the wasteland, leading down to the chilly depths. The scientist and his assistants are trying to gain a greater understanding of both surface and underwater aspects of life near the North Pole.

Charles remembers his dive as follows:

'I lowered myself gingerly into the water, which by now was covered with newly formed pieces of ice—rather like crème de menthe frappe—and sank like a great orange walrus into the ice-covered world below. Once at the bottom of the six-foot shaft the similarity with a walrus vanished abruptly to be replaced by a resemblance to a dirigible balloon underwater. I found it extremely hard to preserve my balance and had to struggle to stay upright.

'Despite the rubber hood, the water felt decidedly cold around my mouth and a few other edges, not to mention the fact that with heavy gloves on my hands I could not get my fingers onto my mask in order to clear my ears. So I ''ballasted'' myself out at a depth which was not too painful and took stock of the situation. It was a fascinating eerie world of greyish-greenish light that met my gaze and above all was the roof of ice which disappeared into the distance.

'The visibility was extraordinarily good. Dr MacInnes said the water was virtually silt-free due to the lack of wave action—the ambient light visibility was 100 feet.'

Under the Arctic ice cap they could die in a minute if their suits were ripped open. Their life lines could be severed, and their oxygen supply could freeze.

This was earthbound man out of his element, very much as he would be on a journey into space. Every second in that incredibly cold water carried the risk of things going wrong. Freezing sea, at four degrees below the level where living flesh turns into a bizarre icicle, could gush into their suits. One of the divers could become disorientated and need to discover a way out of his strange underwater predicament, with solid ice above and just his wits to keep him going.

(Continued on page 11)

After the Prince got used to swimming around in the strange environment, occasionally using his hands to stop him from bumping his head against the underside of the ice pack, he decided to have some fun. Dr MacInnes showed him how to walk upside-down on the roof of ice, with spear-like tails pointing towards them like deadly chandeliers. They floated slowly upwards with weights round their middles so it was like swimming through jelly. They gained the crisp underbelly of the ice cap like people out of a Jacques Cousteau film.

Thrusting their frog-suit flippers with difficulty through the water, they crawled fly-like on a six-foot ceiling of solid ice in a liquid temperature of twenty-eight degrees Fahrenheit.

Talking about his walk later Charles said: 'I could not resist giving it a try! The result was comical in the extreme. I only partly succeeded. What was fascinating was to see the exhaust bubbles from the two of us trapped on the underside of the ice, spread out like great pools of shimmering mercury.'

The icicles? 'They looked like beautiful transparent wafers. Nestling in the gaps between the wafers were lots of shrimp-like creatures.'

His intrepid companion left Prince Charles floating around the craggy undersurface for a few minutes and dived to a shell-shaped station at the bottom of the sea. He returned with a bowler hat on his rubber-capped head, brandishing an umbrella.

The royal frogman reached out, took the umbrella and tried his hand at sub-aqua clowning. He opened the umbrella underwater and posed for pictures with Dr MacInnes.

Now that he was familiar with this jade-coloured underworld he decided to liven up the adventure a little more. He descended sixty feet to the shelter and entered it through an airlock with his fellow swimmer.

Inside he was shown some of the plants growing in a corner of the structure which is being used as a sea-bed laboratory. Then, switching to the surface listening post on the telephone link, Charles and the scientist sang The Beatles' song 'We All Live In a Yellow Submarine'.

When he returned topside he had another trick up his sleeve. In the tent covering the hole carved into the ice he inflated his orange diving suit to amuse the photographers waiting outside. 'The result was astonishing and I looked exactly like M. Michelin,' remembers Charles.

The dive into this weird edge of the world lasted around thirty minutes. Forty minutes is considered to be the limit a first-time diver should stay in these frightening conditions. It was a worrying time for the security men waiting nervously on the surface. No detective would like to go down in history as the man who lost the future King of England—underwater.

To ensure that the Prince's escapade would carry the minimum number of risks, the security team and the diving experts worked out in advance a very careful programme for the operation, which took place 492 nautical miles north of the Arctic Circle. This included a forty-five minute check of the battery-powered heated suit and the other equipment to be used. A rescue team stood by ready to go at the first sign of an emergency.

When he made his 8,000 mile tour around the frozen Northwest Territories he sampled as much as he could of life in the land of the Eskimo.

As soon as he walked down the steps of his plane on to a remote airfield, clad in a natty fur outfit, he was off for a ride on a dog sleigh. He soon got bored with being a passenger. Returning from their six-mile trip over the snow and ice he asked the Eskimo dog handler to sit in the back and took over the huskies.

The first time he came across a snowmobile, he 'went mad', according to one of the party with him. After rapidly learning how to control the half-tracked vehicle he accelerated away, ploughing to the front in a race across the ice. 'He was laughing and shouting like a cowboy on a bucking bronco as he zipped along at around forty-five miles an hour,' said a fellow rider.

Eskimo life fascinated him. He had seen plenty of igloos around and insisted on going inside one of them. It seemed proper to him that he should find out how the most northerly of his future subjects lived.

His hosts also showed him how they built their sparsely furnished dwellings. If an Eskimo is caught in a sudden storm, an igloo is his only protection. Some of them could pile up chunks of ice into an instant home in as little as fifteen minutes.

He watched Eskimos fishing through the ice for seals. A short time later he got more than he had bargained for, however, when he was watching a demonstration of seal-skinning. A young girl came up and offered him the local 'delicacy'—raw seal meat.

'I looked at it and said "Ugh!" but she kept saying I must eat it,' remembers the Prince. 'For the honour of the family I picked up a piece of meat and made the fatal error, of course, of chewing it rather than swallowing it like a sheep's eye.

'The trouble was that it tasted absolutely appalling. I said "The Press here are going to eat this and all the people with me . . . You'll all eat it."

'They shrank away and disappeared. A doctor who was with us muttered in their ears that they shouldn't eat it because it was probably a week old. So I said "Thank you very much chummy, what about me, eh?!"'

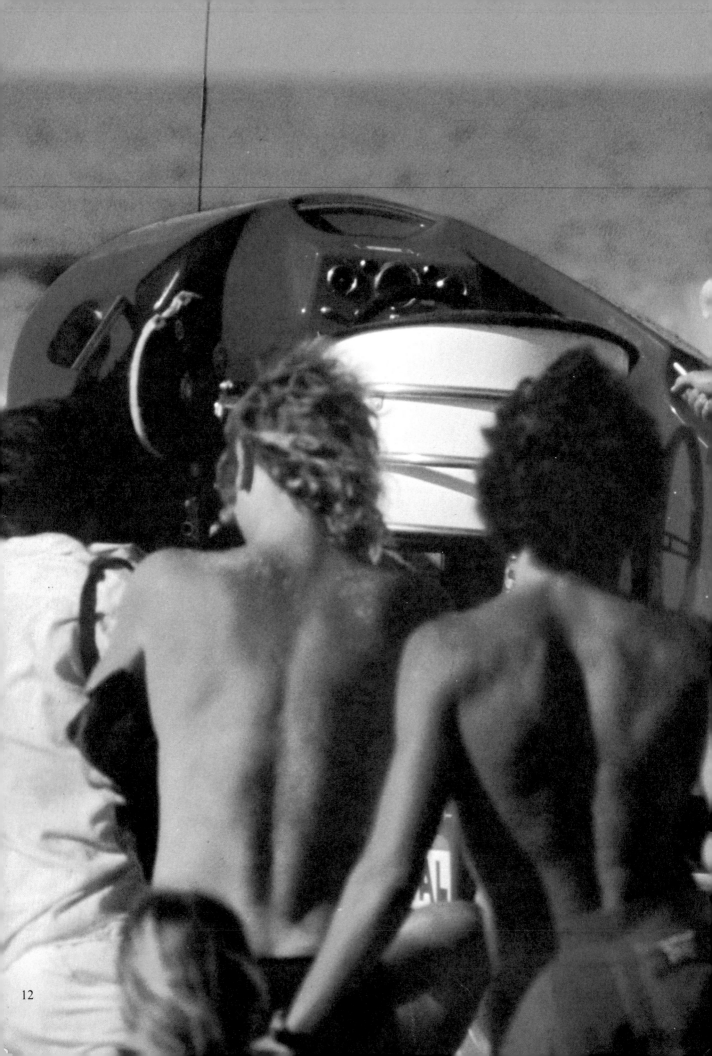

Chapter 2

The People's Prince

Charles, born at Buckingham Palace on the evening of 14 November 1948, is the forty-fourth heir to the throne and the first male in direct succession for more than eighty years. His ancestors include such unlikely figures as the first president of the United States, George Washington, and, according to some, the Prophet of Islam, Mohammed.

As Prince of Wales he is in the ancestral line of a pageant of royalty that includes Edward the Black Prince of the fourteenth century, the marriage-prone Henry VIII, and the man who gave his name to both a style of living and an era, Queen Victoria's son Edward VII.

The only trade Charles has been prepared for is that of kingship. His grandfather, George VI, once said: 'We're not a family, we're a firm.' Already he is a 'junior director' of the enterprise, but unlike most bosses' sons, he cannot easily leave the family business. His role is pre-ordained, unless he wants to cause a constitutional crisis like his late great-uncle the Duke of Windsor, and abdicate.

He will take his throne at a time of changing attitudes toward monarchies. He realises that the days of the aloof king on a golden throne are over, and that the continuation of his own inheritance is being questioned in the Houses of Parliament.

With this in mind he has tried, probably harder than any of his predecessors, to get close to the people he will rule one day. He wants to know how people live and cope in changing societies, what they are thinking—their ambitions, their hates and their loves.

He once admitted he had no idea how people existed in small houses or rented flats, or how they coped on meagre salaries. His understanding is growing because he has constantly sought to meet as many people as possible from all walks of life to learn how they hope to fulfil their ambitions.

Prince Charles says frankly: 'I'm not a normal person in the sense that I was born to be king. I have received a special education and training. I could never be a normal person because I have been prepared to reign over my subjects.'

His popularity at home and abroad shows that he is succeeding in breaking down the barriers between palace and people. At the time of his investiture as Prince of Wales in July 1969, the Mayor of Caernarvon called him 'the ace in the Royal pack'.

Abroad, especially in the Commonwealth countries, his stock with everyone from New Zealand sheepfarmers to Fijian dancing girls seems to rise every year. He is particularly welcome in Australia, one of his favourite places, where he has been given the supreme local tribute of being called a 'ruddy decent Pommy', an accolade that Aussies bestow on few Englishmen!

His links with Australia go back to his schooldays, when he spent a year at Timbertops — the abrasive, open air school in the mountains north of Melbourne. He has returned to Australia regularly ever since. With his love of risking his neck now and again, he goes down well with a people who like a bloke to prove his courage.

The Prince's liking for swimming fits in perfectly with Australia's beach-side way of life. When he paid an official visit in 1974 he spent as much time as possible in the sometimes treacherous, rolling seas.

At Coolangatta, near Cairns, he watched local beach rescue squads in operation in the risky surf. He persuaded the beach guards and anxious local officials to allow him to ride in a powerful new rescue craft. Once in the boat he took over the controls himself, and flew across the waves.

During that tour of Australia and New Zealand he rolled up his sleeves and joined the sheep shearers. These men, who earn their living clipping wool to clothe most of the world's backs, are among the toughest and roughest workers anywhere. Holding hundreds of struggling sheep between your legs every day, and having to reach a seemingly impossible clipping target to earn a decent living, makes the shearers men of hard sinew and muscle.

Charles took to them immediately, and they to him, when he called at a sheep station near Wellington, New Zealand. Their way of life interested him. He asked them about their homes, their families, and what they wanted in the future.

Then the 'gaffer' of the shearers asked Charles to lend a hand. A dozen or so bewildered beasts were brought up and HRH swung into action with a pole, pushing the sheep through a murky, foul-smelling dip. It was a bit of a struggle and he doubted whether he could ever have earned a week's wages on the job. But he learned a little more about one tiny part of his future dominion.

Another trip round this part of the world was made later that year when he went to Fiji. He was guest of honour at the tables of various chiefs in this carefree, natural corner of the Commonwealth. At one function the local chief put two pretty girls on either side of the Prince, changing them every half hour throughout dinner so the royal bachelor would not become bored.

Some of the attractive native women dancers held out their hands and begged Charles to dance with them. Wearing a multicoloured shirt and a garland of flowers he moved onto the dance floor a little gingerly. His dancing companions, with mischievous looks on their faces, and gyrating midriffs, moved faster to the music of the drums.

They danced a complicated local pattern, but the Prince soon got the hang of it and seemed to enjoy joining in the fun. One partner was an especially beautiful girl with a hint of naughtiness in her eyes and movements. It was only afterwards that he realised why. She had trapped him into a traditional island love dance.

Twelve months later he was in the Pacific region again, this time in Papua New Guinea, where the female population is not, by European standards, as attractive as in Polynesia. Charles was confronted one day with a line-up of native girls daubed with vegetable dyes. They were obviously admirable to the young men around them but they were not exactly his type.

He was amused to see two old men prodding and pinching the girls, measuring the dimensions of their faces and examining them like prospective buyers at a cattle sale. The purpose of the whole strange business was then made clear to him. This was a village beauty contest and the head man wanted the visitor he thought would be the most 15

(Continued on page 19)

worthy of all, to be chairman of the judges. Taking a good look at the contestants, Charles turned to his hosts and, as delicately as possible, declined the honour.

Dipping a royal foot into the whirlpool of life can be amusing but it also has its more frightening and discomforting aspects. These the Prince has had to undergo as part of his training in the Royal Navy and Royal Air Force.

Such experiences included a practice submarine underwater escape from 100 feet down, without any breathing apparatus. Men have died doing the same thing in the Royal Navy's training tank at *HMS Dolphin* at Gosport in Hampshire. The Prince had to go through with it to prepare himself for a nuclear submarine patrol.

After 'escaping' from depths of thirty, then sixty feet without breathing equipment, he descended to the base of the practice tank, filled with 700 tons of sea water. Wearing a protective suit, goggles and a clip over his nose he stepped into an airlock which was a mock-up of the sort found in submarines.

A connecting door was opened and water began to pour in. When it reached his neck Charles took a deep breath and entered the base of the tank. As the natural buoyancy in his body took

17

Visiting a New Zealand sheep farm

him upwards he had to remember to breathe out carefully, 'whistling to the top' as the experts call it. If he had not done this his lungs could have been damaged under the tremendous water pressure or an air-bubble might have been forced into his bloodstream, causing a blockage in the heart.

He kept a cool head, remembered all his instructors had taught him, and shot out of the water at the top of the tank like a cork.

Part of his training as a helicopter pilot involved taking part in what the Royal Marine Commandos call a 'Tarzan' course. As a Royal Navy pilot he has to carry the commandos, so the Admiralty thought it was a good idea for him and other pilots to get first-hand knowledge of what the Green Berets do. A group of pilots went through the ordeal of a gruelling commando endurance test at the Royal Marine training centre at Lympstone in Devon.

He scaled climbing nets and vertical walls, edged along catwalks, swung across chasms, slid down ropes at death-defying speeds and crawled from tree to tree on a swaying rope-walk. Then came a mile and a half cross-country slog followed by an even tougher military refinement. He had to crawl through tunnels half-filled with water and one completely filled. At the other end of this one the strong arms of a marine were waiting to pull him through by the scruff of his neck.

19

After all the training: Charles as Colonel of the Welsh Guards at home *(opposite)*, in Ghana *(above)* and in Papua New Guinea *(right)*

With typical British understatement, the only judgement the Royal Marines would allow themselves after the marathon performance was: 'The Prince showed he didn't lack physical fitness.'

During his earlier RAF training, Charles made a parachute jump from a twin-engined Andover of the RAF Support Command over the English Channel, down to a bay on the Dorset coast. When the plane was in position, at an altitude of 1,200 feet, a sliding door opened near the tail and the whistle of the slipstream could be heard. Below, the sea looked a long way down.

The despatcher nodded to Prince Charles that he should get ready and walk to the edge of the heaving doorway. He stood up, steadying himself to get his balance. The static line that would, hopefully, pull out his 'chute as he left the plane was attached to a cable. He checked his reserve 'chute, strapped on the front of his blue flying overalls, and the quick release catch. The despatcher, Flight Sergeant Ken Kidd, thought he was a little too far from the door, and suggested a few steps forward might be in order.

With less than a minute to go the Andover began its final run over Studland Bay, a holiday beach near Poole. The Prince gripped the side of the exit. A green light went on and Kidd tapped him on the shoulder and shouted 'Go!' Charles jumped without hesitation. With a welcome jerk the Prince felt the canopy open, but then something went wrong and he found himself descending with his legs caught in the rigging.

He kept his cool as he dropped towards splashdown and now recounts the incident objectively: 'I determined to myself that I wouldn't think about the jump too much beforehand. Otherwise I would have worried. In the end I stood in the doorway and I didn't need kicking out. I jumped out happily except that after I'd jumped, for some unknown reason—I must have hollow legs or something—my legs went over my head.

'The next thing I knew they were tangled in the rigging lines, so I was looking up at them and coming down in a sort of U shape. I said to myself calmly "Your legs are in the rigging so you must remove them." So I removed them—fortunately —by about 800 feet. Then I had a lovely sail down to sea level. Of course I forgot to inflate my life jacket because I'd enjoyed it so much.'

When he hit the sea, motor launches, manned by Royal Marines, fished him out of the water within ten seconds and whisked him away for a stiff drink.

This is the man who will inherit one of the oldest crowns in the world. The successor to a monarchy that goes back 1,500 years to a Saxon warrior king called Cedric, and a descendant who commands the greatest universal respect.

Chapter 3
It Can Be Fun

'Treat 'em mean and keep 'em keen' just about sums up the hardy old-seadog philosophy of Britannia Royal Naval College, Dartmouth. It is a view of life shared by the officers on the staff who deal out a formidable amount of that meanness. *Britannia,* or the 'Stone Frigate' as she has

been called by generations of naval officers who have suffered on her parade ground, lies among the flower-beds and green acres alongside the River Dart in Devon.

The primary task of the college is to lick into shape the successors to Nelson. It has been the finishing school for future British kings for almost a century; they go there to submit to harsh discipline and have their teenage corners knocked off them.

Prince Charles' ancestors for more than a century have had to go through it. His father Prince Philip, his grandfather George VI and his great-grandfather George V—'the sailor king'—all had the final touches of royal lustre painfully varnished on them there. Charles has had to brace up to it in his turn.

King George V insisted in his day that a spell before the mast was essential for young princes to prepare themselves for royal duties. Prince Charles also supports this view. On one occasion towards the end of his career at sea he said: 'I feel that if one is going to get involved in the whole spectrum of life in this country, then one should get to know about the Services. One should get to know about the Navy particularly because ultimately our security and everything depends upon the Navy. It always has done throughout history and always will. Therefore it is very important to know about it. Having learnt at school that discipline exists, and being highly disciplined myself, helped me in the Navy.'

Charles went to Dartmouth in the late summer of 1971 to prepare himself for the five years he was to spend as a Royal Navy officer in what will one day be his King's Navy, to learn at every level from bridge to lower deck the operations and the cherished legends of Britain's senior Service.

He had already served at the Royal Air Force College, Cranwell, where he won his wings and graduated from Cambridge University with a Bachelor of Arts degree. Because of these qualifications he did not have to join the Navy as an ordinary cadet. As an acting sub-lieutenant the Prince of Wales was among a dozen university graduate officers who 'went aboard' *Britannia* to take a crammed six-week course before going into various branches of the Royal Navy.

He had a twelve-hour non-stop day from early morning until dusk. Before seven each morning his steward Joseph Atkinson woke him up with just enough time to reach breakfast in the sub-lieutenants' mess. Mr Atkinson kept the Prince's cabin tidy, but the young officer had to polish his own shoes and keep his clothes and uniforms smart.

Charles and the other officers barely had time to swallow their breakfasts before being put through their paces in half an hour of marching

Charles with his helicopter instructor

and gymnastics. The man in charge of the 'square bashing', Lieutenant Peter Richardson, said at the time: 'We have no special attitude towards graduates. They get kicked to death like any other man. But I think most people enjoy it. It can be fun.'

With just a short time available the instructors tried to make the Prince and his classmates worthy of command. On the parade ground there were three hour-long sessions each week in addition to the daily parades, including marching, standing to attention, saluting, and, even in the age of nuclear submarines, sword drill.

In the gymnasium there were at least two hour-long sessions every week, planned, according to one of the sports officers, 'so that one reaches the limit of one's endurance in a very short space of time.' For his first swimming test, Charles had to swim 400 metres in a boiler suit, float for three minutes, then dive to the bottom of the college

pool and pick up a brick nearly eight feet down. He also learned life saving and how to give mouth-to-mouth resuscitation on a bionde Swedish dummy known to the cadets as 'Resusci-Anne'.

But most of the busy days were spent in classrooms learning the text-book techniques of life at sea, and studying navigation, weaponry, marine and electrical engineering, administration and management.

It was rough going, but in the end Prince Charles got through his first major test as a naval officer. Under a dull sky on the last Friday of October 1971, he and his fellow graduate officers led the passing out parade of 500 officer cadets while the band played, appropriately, 'God Bless the Prince of Wales'.

Watching with pride was Charles' great-uncle, Admiral of the Fleet Earl Mountbatten of Burma. This famous naval figure and World War II leader had always been among those members of the Royal Family who wanted the Prince to 'go away to sea'.

The Royal Navy has been a career that Charles enjoyed, although it was a profession practised for only a brief time because of the other demands of apprentice kingship. Thanks to the family tradition the Royal Navy and the rewards of serving in it meant a great deal to him. His time there gave the Navy a chance to get to know him, while he had the opportunity of meeting some of his future subjects at close quarters. There are few secrets in some of the tiny ships he has served in. He got used to living closely with people from totally different backgrounds and social classes to his own.

'You're all together out there at sea, cut off, in that small community,' he said. 'It's a very intense communal life.'

He might have been a prince ashore, but during his naval duties he appeared on ships' crew lists as either Sub-lieutenant, or later Lieutenant Charles Windsor. As such he received the same treatment and workload as any other officer, including those exhausting nightly 'dog watches'. As a junior officer he became responsible for the welfare, as well as discipline, of as many as thirty men under him.

This included helping them sort out their personal problems, whether they were debts, trouble with girl friends, or worries about their marriages; he could even have had the sad task of telling a man that a relative had died.

'Where else could a future king learn how difficult it is to keep a wife and family together during long separations and on a limited budget?' pointed out one of his captains.

He soon got the hang of getting on with the seamen he commanded. After five weeks at sea in his first ship, the County class guided missile destroyer *HMS Norfolk*, he came ashore at

29

Part of his submarine escape training

Portsmouth dockyard for a few days leave. A rating who, like the rest of the 400 men on board, had been watching closely the way the newcomer found his sea legs said: 'The lads like him. He listens to you . . . you don't think of him as royalty,' and added, 'He's a good shipmate!'

The 'good shipmate' also showed he could mix socially with the greatest of ease when he went to the *Norfolk's* annual dance, an occasion very special to the crew; a big night out ashore with all their wives and girl friends. A familiar face among the crush at the local Palais de Danse in Portsmouth was Prince Charles. Wearing his sub-lieutenant's uniform, he danced with the wives of fellow officers and ratings and dipped his hand into his pocket to stand his round of drinks.

The three years following that marching out parade at Dartmouth were mainly spent at sea, in a great variety of ships, learning the trade of being a naval officer in all parts of the world. He gained his watch-keeping certificate—the Navy's 'driving licence'—during the total of nine months that he was on the *Norfolk*. This qualified him to be in complete charge of a ship, responsible for every decision he took as officer-of-the-watch on the bridge.

During those three years, and during all his time at sea, he was spared none of the duties the other officers had to carry out. Yet, at the same time, he still had his royal functions. He had to study State papers, stored in specially secure safes in his various cabins, keep up with the administration of his estates as Duke of Cornwall, and handle the usual heavy load of royal correspondence.

While other officers could relax in the wardroom, he caught up with briefings on State affairs, read reports and recommendations from his staff at Buckingham Palace or the London offices of the Duchy of Cornwall, and considered the hundreds of requests received every year, from all kinds of organisations and societies, for his royal patronage.

Whenever his ship reached port, there would usually be a bag of official papers waiting for him at the end of the gangplank. There would also be one of his armed private detectives, who had flown ahead of him. The Royal Navy was expected to look after the future king at sea, but, in this unpredictable age of assassins, there was always tight security ashore. Away from the freedom of life at sea, he became once more a royal personage, one of the privileged few, a man of power and, therefore, a potential target.

Charles, like other members of his family, often receives threats to his life. Most of them are ignored, while a few have to be taken seriously. In these cases Scotland Yard's Special Branch makes a few discreet enquiries about the crank who has got a grudge against the Prince. When the Royal

Family visits any part of Britain, security checks are made on people living locally who have threatened foul deeds. They are then put under unobtrusive surveillance.

On trips abroad the local police usually carry out the same rigid procedures at the request of the Yard. But the public as a whole, and the many people who come close to the Queen and her family, cannot all be screened by the security people. Opportunities for a sudden attack on the members of the Royal Family have become greater in recent years because of their habit of going on 'walkabouts' among crowds. Charles is particularly fond of mixing in with the people, as he once showed while chatting to women and children in a stroll around the streets of Windsor. It was a security man's nightmare — anyone in the crowd could have assaulted him.

The threat of an assassination attempt is always there—a danger that Charles has experienced at least once in a violent and dramatic way, when a naval officer attacked him one night while he was asleep.

It happened in April 1974, shortly after Princess Anne and her husband Captain Mark Phillips were held at gunpoint in the Mall during a fruitless single-handed kidnap attempt. At the time Charles was a lieutenant on the frigate *HMS Jupiter,* which had just returned to Plymouth after a world cruise. He was away from the ship taking a course on under-water warfare at Portland, Dorset, and had been allocated quarters ashore in RN barracks.

Around two o'clock in the morning, the Prince was awakened by a sound in the sitting room adjoining his bedroom. As he opened the connecting door he saw a figure rushing towards him.

His attacker and the Prince began to struggle in the darkness. The other man picked up a chair and was about to smash it over Charles' head when he was grabbed from behind. Charles' rescuer was Inspector Paul Officer, one of the royal bodyguards who had been sleeping in a nearby bedroom.

Having heard shouts and furniture being knocked over, the burly 6ft 2in detective burst in on the grappling pair, and he and Charles overpowered the man.

Within minutes they were joined by RN Police and, screaming and yelling, the intruder was dragged away. He turned out to be another lieutenant who had suddenly become mentally unbalanced. A secret enquiry was made into the incident and the man was committed to a Service hospital.

A doctor was called to examine Charles and although he was shaken, he suffered nothing more serious than slight bruising.

Because this happened in a top-security Service establishment, well away from the public, it was easy for the authorities to hush up the incident, and a black-out on information was imposed.

One of the sad lessons for Charles and the men responsible for protecting him was that they could never be too careful in future. Previously it had always been thought that while he was in the Navy, surrounded by well-disciplined crew, he was in one of the safest possible situations.

Now even this had a high-risk factor. Security afloat and ashore was tightened up, and Charles and his detectives rehearsed how to react to various forms of attack. They studied and practised how and where Charles would dodge, dive and weave, faced with gunmen, bombs or straightforward physical violence.

Despite this ever-present danger ashore, and the extra royal work afloat, he managed to collect a kit-bag full of happy memories and adventures in the *Jupiter,* his fourth ship. He went halfway round the world in this 2,450 ton Leander class frigate, flying first to join her in the Far East, then sailing across the Pacific to the West Coast of America and through the Panama Canal for the return Atlantic journey to Britain.

31

In RN tropical uniform in Ghana *(top);*
Colonel of the Welsh Guards in Papua New Guinea *(bottom)*

For a large part of his four months on board he was the radio officer, but he also took his turn on the bridge, with the responsibility of watch-keeping. He was not long out from Singapore one stormy day in the South Java Sea when he helped to rescue the twelve-man crew of a tug in distress.

While he was manning the bridge the radio room picked up SOS signals from the stricken Singapore tug *Mediator,* which had gone aground in the storm. Prince Charles ordered a change of course to the scene and alerted the skipper, Commander John Gunning, who joined him on the bridge. The captain backed the young officer's decision and sent off the ship's tiny Wasp helicopter on a search sortie in the driving rain. The pilot, Lieutenant Lawrence Hopkins, spotted the tug and its two barges being battered in the foul weather.

It needed seven airborne attempts to put a boarding party on the tug and send over towing barges. After four hours of dangerous, tough work in the sort of tempestuous conditions Conrad would have written about, the *Jupiter* and its crew freed the vessels and pulled them to a safe anchorage.

Such was the anonymity of Charles as just another officer doing his job that it is doubtful even today that those twelve men realise how a royal hand came to their rescue.

By this time he had been promoted—he was Lieutenant Charles Windsor. The crew had, however, given the Prince of Wales another name—'Taffy Windsor'.

When the *Jupiter* reached the other side of the Pacific and was taking part in exercises with the United States Navy in California's San Diego Bay, the Welsh lieutenant saved the ship from what could have been a disastrous collision with another frigate.

He was navigating officer, keeping a close watch on the radar in thick fog, when he spotted the blip of the other ship on the screen heading straight towards the *Jupiter.* The other vessel was the *USS Grindley,* an American-style 'frigate' more than twice the size and weight of the British warship. Charles flashed off urgent signals and, with hasty manoeuvring, the two missed each other by forty feet.

When the *Jupiter* reached Plymouth the naval career of Prince Charles took a new direction. Those months at sea enviously watching the Wasp anti-submarine helicopter buzzing around had revived his old flying bug. If he was to specialise in any one branch of the Royal Navy, he had already made up his mind that the Fleet Air Arm was for him.

His interest in flying had been encouraged early by his father. Charles was twenty when he first went solo in a single-engine, propeller-driven Chipmunk, emblazoned in red—the colour of the

Queen's Flight, that elite squadron of the Royal Air Force. He had an immediate aptitude for flying and the men who have accompanied him in the cockpits of many aircraft since then—from the comparatively snail-like Chipmunk to supersonic Phantom fighter bombers—have all agreed that he is a 'natural' airman.

Like every pilot who has had to face up to the final terrifying test of going solo, Prince Charles remembers that moment well. 'It's imprinted on my mind indelibly. I suppose I worried about it for a bit . . . the thought of actually having to go solo and whether I was capable of doing it. Whether I'd remember the right things to do.

'But when the day came,the instructor got out of the cockpit, rather surprisingly as I didn't think I was going to do it that day, and said "Right—it's your turn!" So I sat there with butterflies in my tummy while he got out and then when I was actually airborne I was amazed how much more fun it was.

'I flew round and round and admired the scenery. I controlled my butterflies. Then I did a perfect landing as it turned out—I never did a better one after that.'

From that day onwards, just like his father, flying had got into his blood. He could not get enough of it and a spell in the Royal Air Force was inevitable. He wanted to hear the roar of the jet engines and feel the G-force pinning him in his seat in a tight aerobatic turn.

Prince Charles joined the RAF at twenty-three. He went to Cranwell, the Air Force College in Lincolnshire which has been the training ground for top pilots for nearly fifty years.

He was able to jump the queue somewhat in the Royal Air Force as he did later in the Navy and only had to go through a streamlined, speeded-up course. As a graduate qualified pilot, he was gazetted as a Flight Lieutenant before he set foot in the college. He carried the rings of rank on the sleeves of his uniform as he flew to Cranwell to be inducted into the service.

With perhaps forgivable ostentation, he piloted himself there in a twin-engine, Bassett light aircraft of the Queen's Flight.

Waiting for him, apart from a line-up of top RAF brass, was a five-month programme which would bring out in him that excellence needed to qualify for wings in the Royal Air Force. The senior officers who greeted him made it clear that he was going to have to earn his wings. A true case of 'per ardua ad astra'—by hard work to reach the stars.

The operation to get the royal pilot to supersonic level was code-named 'Exercise Golden Eagle'. He became part of the first course made up entirely of university graduates, sharing a flat with three other ex-student cadets and like them he was subject to Service discipline.

Charles on helicopter training

Heading towards the stratosphere was Charles' ambition, but before he was allowed to go aloft in one of the two specially maintained Provost jet trainers, he had to go through a gruelling test on the ground. He was locked in a decompression chamber, 'taken up' to 20,000 feet in simulated conditions—then he unhooked his oxygen mask.

The effect of this is just like the moment before blacking out in the dentist's chair, after being given a whiff of anaesthetic. A pilot becomes drowsy and quite loses his bearings before feeling himself disappear into a void. Charles had to experience this in the testing chamber so he would recognise the symptoms if his oxygen supply went wrong while he was in the air.

During this oxygen training at an aero-medical training centre not far from Cranwell he had to leave his mask off for several minutes and do simple handwriting tests until he was on the verge of a blackout. What he wrote during this highly uncomfortable experiment is rumoured to be in language appropriate to the discomfort of the time. It is a choice piece of memorabilia which the RAF has tucked safely away for historical purposes.

Although it was not his wish, the Air Force went to incredible lengths to make sure Charles got through his flying course safely. Radar kept his aircraft under constant surveillance when he was flying, and other aircraft for fifty miles around Cranwell were ordered to keep clear. A maintenance team twice the usual size made sure that the two 480mph Provost trainers, earmarked for him, were always in faultless condition. In addition his planes had special red flashing lights fitted to distinguish them from other trainers.

The Junior Service did its best, but the Prince presented them with a major problem that only he could solve. One of the essential qualities for any pilot is a ready understanding of mathematics. Charles, unfortunately has always been towards the bottom of the class when it came to mental arithmetic and rapid calculation in such boring pastimes as algebraic equations, geometric formulae and logarithmic tables, a blind spot he shares with the Queen.

As he is the first to admit: 'Maths taken in its pure context is misery I think. I find it boring. I'm one of those people who prefers ideas rather than numbers. I could never understand maths. I always thought it was the way I'd been taught originally that made me so hopeless, but, on the other hand, perhaps I just don't have a mathematical mind.'

Prince royal or not, a pilot without some skill in mathematics was of no use to the Royal Air Force. He just had to get up to scratch. He put his head down and, fighting his way through a battlefield of unfriendly figures, managed to reach a maths standard that satisfied his instructors. Even today though, he says with remarkable honesty: 'From the flying point of view my arithmetic is not as fast as some other people's.'

Once in the cockpit of a jet trainer, with the controls in his hands, the natural talent he has above zero feet flashed through. He quickly got the hang of flying jets and was soon learning the aerobatics needed by a jet-age fighter pilot. He made his first solo flight after only eight hours' instruction instead of the usual ten.

The Prince wanted to get a taste of all the aircraft being flown by the RAF during the short time he would be able to spend in the Service. With his excellent record as a pilot to back him up, he could make a good claim to get his hands on the more exotic hardware.

Such aircraft as the McDonnel F-4M

Taking his first command, *HMS Bronington,* at Rosyth in Scotland

Phantom, for example. It is what Americans would call a 'hot one'— capable of flying at twice the speed of sound, rocketing up to nearly 100,000 feet in just over six minutes, and outflying and outshooting most adversaries in the world. It is one of Britain's main lines of defence.

Just a few weeks after he had gone solo, Charles co-piloted a Phantom of Forty-three—'The Fighting Cocks' squadron from Leuchars in Scotland. He took part in a scramble and an interception over the North Sea with another Phantom acting as 'the enemy', then his aircraft nudged in carefully behind a Victor flyer tanker to take on 1,200 gallons of fuel—one of the hairiest of airborne manoeuvres. Few pilots like doing this because of the risks of an explosive collision.

He flew as high as 40,000 feet and as low as 1,000 feet when he made a pass over the Royal Family's summer house at Balmoral in a final flourish. When he landed he was made a member of the exclusive Ten Ton Club—that enviable group who have piloted a plane at more than 1,000 mph.

The next day he sat in a more spacious cockpit, alongside the captain of a Nimrod maritime reconnaissance aircraft, for a day-long patrol over the Atlantic. For four hours he piloted this four-engined jet whose main function is the detection, and in wartime, the destruction of submarines. With sophisticated radar and underwater search equipment, just one Nimrod can monitor the surface and undersea movements of the entire Mediterranean in a few high-flying minutes.

The Prince then rounded off his tropospheric

education a week later in a nuclear bomber. He co-piloted a Vulcan, the delta-wing aircraft that is the mainstay of the British strategic strike force. With four powerful engines it travels at just under the speed of sound with a frightening destructive capability of either missiles, hydrogen bombs or 21,000 pounds worth of what are chillingly called 'conventional' bombs.

The citizens of Doncaster, with its famous race-course in South Yorkshire, were not aware of it at the time, but they had the privilege of being the target when their future king made a high-level dummy attack on them.

It was to be another five years, after his naval service, before he got the chance to fly a jet again. He went back to Cranwell in February 1977—now a Wing Commander—to brush up his basic flying and aerobatics.

'I've forgotten so much,' he said. 'Especially those convolutions of the stomach when you go into a roll or a loop. Dangerous? No, it's more dangerous crossing the road.'

For his helicopter training, Charles joined the aptly named Red Dragon flight of Number 707 naval squadron at Yeovilton in Somerset. He was trained to handle one of the most difficult aircraft to fly, the big twin-engine Wessex helicopters.

For three and a half months he worked hard at getting the hang of controlling and navigating a Wessex in all weathers and over any type of terrain. Mountain flying was the most difficult and the most hazardous. He did this among the peaks of his own principality of Wales, actually landing on top of Mount Snowdon.

He trained in air-sea rescue work, learning to manoeuvre just above wave tops, blinded by the spray his own rotors were throwing up, in order to winch volunteers to safety from the water. Charles was also taught how to fire weapons such as rockets and guided missiles, and how to take commandos into battle.

After 105 flying hours, spread over forty-five days, he went solo and qualified as an operational helicopter combat pilot—ready for anything, anywhere in the world.

Red Dragon flight became a front line squadron on board the commando carrier *HMS Hermes*. Charles and the rest of the newly trained pilots were taken to the other side of the Atlantic. They flew in the sub-tropical temperatures of the Caribbean and below zero in Northern Canada.

Helicopter flying became the greatest thrill of his life. He said at the time: 'It's very challenging. There's that superb mixture of fear and enjoyment which comes over me.

'It is marvellous when things are going right and you can pick up a reference on the ground and not bother with the map. Then that panic when you don't really know where you are and you've got to sort it out yourself. It's so exciting.

'I've given myself a fright or two. The other day we were going along quite well when flames suddenly started to shoot out of the engine on my side, making extraordinary "whoof-whoof" noises. All the instruments were twitching away.

'Fortunately, I was with the senior pilot of the squadron so we shut down the engine and landed in a ploughed field beside a motorway—much to everybody's amazement!'

On another occasion though he admitted 'It's bloody terrifying sometimes.'

Charles had been allowed to spend five years in the Royal Navy, until he reached the level of being the captain of his own ship. In the New Year of 1976 he was eventually given his own command, after studying at the Navy's senior 'university', the Royal Naval College, Greenwich.

With Britain's small navy of today there are few ships of any size around to put in the hands of a prince. In the end Charles became the skipper of one of the smallest ships in the fleet, *HMS Bronington*.

The 360 ton *Bronington*—named after a Welsh village—is a wooden-hulled minehunter. When Charles joined her she had such a bad reputation for unsteadiness because of her flat bottom that she was said to 'roll on wet grass'. Her nickname in the service is 'Old Quarter-past-eleven'—her pennant number is 1115.

During his ten months on board he often had great difficulty controlling the ship in even the slightest hint of bad weather. She became the only ship in his entire naval career to make him seasick, a malady he can claim to have shared with Nelson.

She was so tough to handle that when he docked her at Rosyth after his first ten weeks at sea as skipper he said: 'They took ten years off my life . . . I feel about eighty.'

The *Bronington* was a workhorse, given the tasks that the larger vessels could not be bothered with. Charles took her minehunting, and blew up the odd mine. For two days he shadowed a Russian submarine caught prowling around Britain's coast.

He zig-zagged among the super-tankers and large cargo vessels passing through the world's busiest—and riskiest—seaway, the Straits of Dover. He was there to check on 'rogue' skippers who were not keeping to the navigation rules.

He took part in NATO exercises, bringing his 36-man crew to battle stations against mock attacks by 'Russian ships'.

Charles, with his sense of humour and fine skill at getting on with people, was a popular skipper. When he gave up his command at the end of 1976 he had a rousing send-off from his shipmates. They hung a black polished lavatory seat round his neck with *'HMS Bronington'* inscribed on it in gold letters, to remind him of the weight of the throne!

Opposite: Charles and Inspector Officer, the man who saved his life

Charles and favourite girlfriend Lady Sarah Spencer

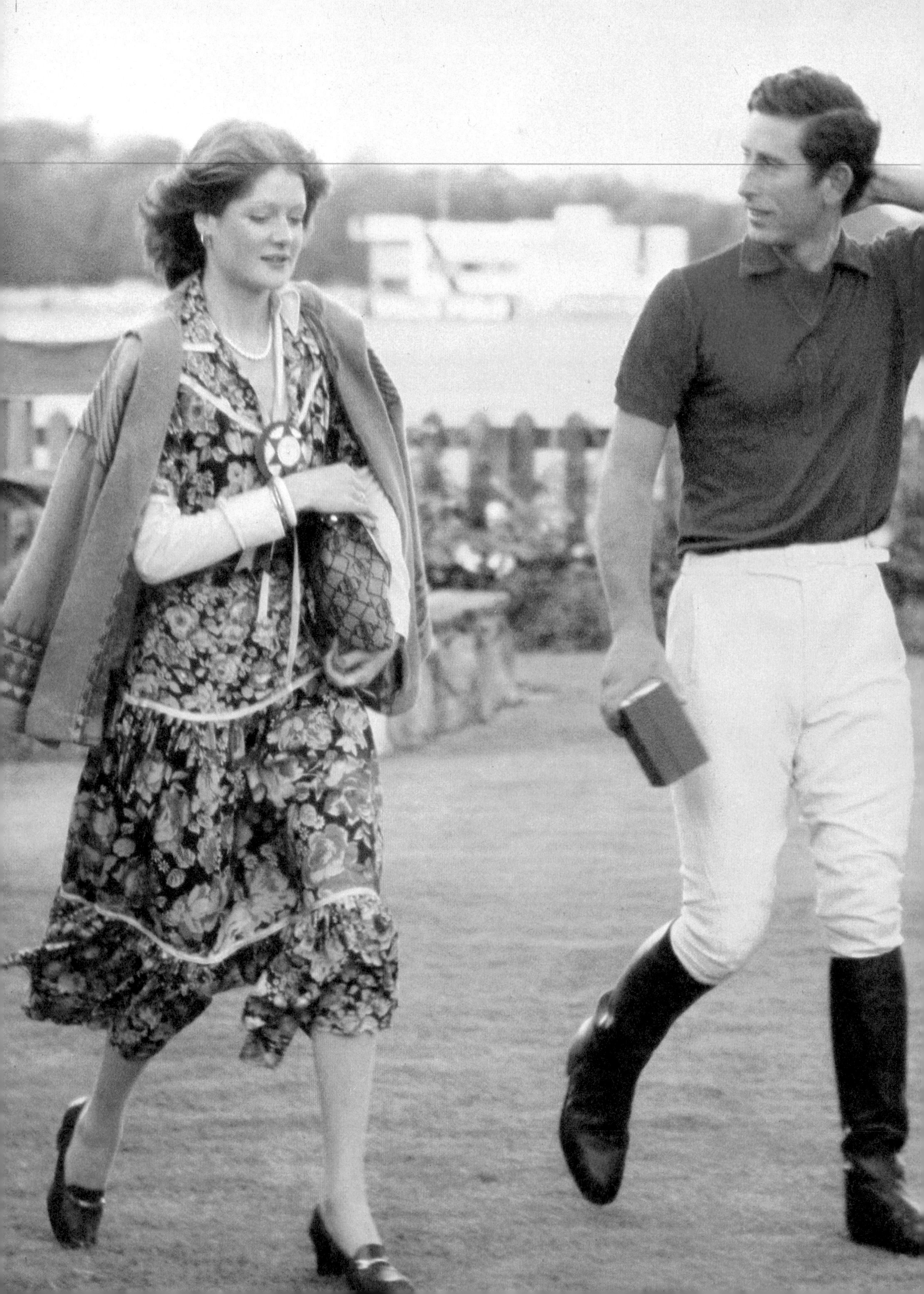

Chapter 4
The Next Queen

There has been wide-spread speculation about Prince Charles and his girlfriends. The teenager who tended to look like a plum pudding has grown into an attractive man. He is an elegant and eligible bachelor with a disarming smile, easy gentle manner and a friendly glint in his eyes. He has been seen with many lovely ladies but most have escaped the gossip columns.

He is particularly discreet with anyone he really cares about and meetings take place well off the beaten track, sometimes in a trustworthy friend's house. He has a private retreat in the Scilly Isles for example, where he can relax away from the public eye.

He frequently shows his appreciation of women. During his successful tour of Fiji, as he was about to depart from a village in a Land Rover, an outstandingly beautiful dancer, clad in a bikini top and grass skirt, beckoned to him.

Although he was surrounded by the usual entourage of officials, and watched by hundreds of people, he walked over to the girl who draped a garland round his neck and kissed him. He put his hands on her waist and returned her embrace. He kissed her again and from the happy look on his face he obviously enjoyed the encounter.

There may be some regal advisers at Buckingham Palace who disapprove of a future king embracing a South Seas dancing girl but their views are unlikely to influence Charles.

(Continued on page 46)

Performing a love dance in Fiji
with another beautiful dancer
Overleaf: With The Queen and
Lady Sarah on a polo outing

During one official Pacific tour he just took off with a girl to a small, deserted, palm-tree covered island. His blonde partner was Jeanette Stinson, the 23-year-old daughter of Fiji's Minister of Finance, Mr Charles Stinson. They sneaked off to the remote island of Vomo, where they walked across the white sand together, played around in the surf and sunbathed under the blazing sun.

Jeanette had first met Charles two years earlier when he visited the area in *HMS Jupiter*. She said later: 'We are friends but it would be wrong to call me a girlfriend.'

Having a strong, wicked sense of humour, Charles sometimes goes to great lengths to be seen with fun-loving girls who are willing to be decoys, drawing attention away from the girls who really feature in his life.

The American admiral's daughter Laura Jo Watkins, who was briefly seen around with the Prince in 1974, was, according to some of his friends, brought on the scene to take the heat off that year's romance with Lady Jane Wellesley. Blonde and college-girl pretty, Laura Jo did not mind. She told the folks back home: 'I had a fantastic time.'

The Prince has always said that he would get married when he was 'around thirty' and he has very down-to-earth views about committing himself.

His marriage must be for keeps, without any question of subsequent divorce. He regards it as a frightening decision because of the special need, in his case, to find the right partner to live with in harmony.

'I hope I will be as lucky as my own parents who have been so happy,' he once said.

He told an interviewer: 'Marriage is a much more important business than falling in love. I think it is essentially a question of mutual love and respect for each other. Creating a secure family unit in which to bring up children and give them a happy, secure upbringing, that is what marriage is all about—creating a home.'

His bride will have to learn much more than just wife-craft. She will have to pick up the royal trade, manners and protocol. She will have to relinquish much and expect very little freedom in her private life. She will be a prisoner of palaces, held in the grasp of royal duties.

Princess Anne's betrothal to Captain Mark Phillips, a commoner, brought Charles a double joy. One was because of the natural love he has for his sister, but the other pleasure came from the fact that his new brother-in-law did not come from the international royals.

The acceptance of a commoner by the Royal Family, the Government and the people of Britain and the Commonwealth, widened the choice available to Charles. He could decide on someone who was not born to the sound of saluting guns.

When he has cast his eyes around the world's palaces he has had precious little to choose from. There is a dearth of princesses waiting in their ivory towers for Charles to come whirling in by helicopter and whizz them away. There are hardly any in the same age group or with the same interests as the British prince.

A few tentative steps were taken by Prince Rainier and Princess Grace of Monaco to push forward Princess Caroline as a suitable partner a few years ago, but this came to nothing. When

Charles met Caroline at the Variety Club gala in Monte Carlo in the early summer of 1977 he jested: 'I've only met the girl once and they are trying to marry us off.'

They water-skied, dined in some of the world's most elegant salons and generally tasted the delights of the Cote d'Azur, but eventually it became clear that nuptials were not what they or their families had in mind. The beautiful princess returned to her sophisticated life among the stylish 'Tout Paris'—and another romance—while the prince flew away to London to the more mundane job of helping to organise his mother's Silver Jubilee celebrations.

Any girl from the ranks would still have to be from a good family, well-educated, and have an unshakeable sense of duty. Knowing his taste in girls she would also have to be a good horsewoman, an excellent swimmer, enjoy an outdoor life, have an interest in music and a taste for adventure, and share his sense of humour. She does not have to be a classic beauty. She needs to be attractive and presentable, more than an absolute stunner. Her clothes will be in delicate good taste, not flamboyant, although he is not noted for his awareness of what a girlfriend is wearing.

These qualities were what attracted the Prince

(Continued on page 52)

49

Charles in Australia with his former secretary Rosemary Taylor

to the blonde and lovely Davina Sheffield, the ex-debutante daughter of an army major. Davina and Charles first became involved with each other when Davina spent part of her summer holiday with the Royal Family at Balmoral. But four months later they broke up.

Davina rather dramatically left London and headed for Vietnam, offering her services to international relief organisations. Because she had no nursing or medical training she could not get the sort of work she wanted to do among the sick and wounded. She did, however, find something worthwhile to do. She looked after sixty abandoned or orphaned youngsters in a rundown Saigon house. It was tough going, in miserable surroundings.

When the Viet Cong began to take over the country and infiltrate into the southern capital she hung on for as long as possible before fleeing to Thailand just days before the Communist take-over.

She told friends in Saigon who were trying to persuade her to leave before it was too late: 'I feel a real sense of purpose here and don't want to leave.'

From Bangkok she went to Australia for a short while before returning to England and another meeting with Charles. Their mutual friends were delighted to see the two of them together again. He gave formal acknowledgment of his feelings for her by producing Davina in public once more as his glamorous and laughing companion during polo at Smith's Lawn, Windsor.

During that long summer they spent more and more time together. Whenever he could get ashore from his naval duties he would be with Davina at some quiet country retreat, dining with just a few close friends, or having her meet his family again.

Occasionally they would speed away in his 140mph Aston Martin Volante to what was once a secluded beach for surfing at Bantham, near Kingsbridge, Devon. This seclusion ended when Davina was caught in the nude in the men's changing room. She did not bat an eyelid when confronted by the local beach guard, but word spread around about the couple's visits to the place and one more secret trysting place had to be crossed off their list.

For three months in 1976, while Charles was mostly at sea skippering his minesweeper, they did not see each other. But by September they were hand-in-hand again.

Davina comes from landed gentry stock and she is a cousin of Lord McGowan, one of the newer baronetcies. Vivacious, intelligent, warm and sensitive, with a ready wit, Davina was a suitably well brought up young 'gel', fit for an English prince.

Apart from the terrible scenes she witnessed in South East Asia, she also knew tragedy in her own life. Her widowed 62-year-old mother was murdered, battered to death, early in 1976 at the family mansion at Ramsden in Oxfordshire.

Prince Charles' natural sympathy for anyone in distress was a great help to her during the months she tried to get over her grief.

Obviously some of his girlfriends have meant a great deal to the Prince, but many have been fleeting fancies. Few of those young ladies who claimed they had something special going for them with the heir apparent, or who were gossiped about, really did have close romantic ties with him. But there have been others beside Davina whose friendship Charles has valued greatly.

One of his first romantic ties was made while he was at Cambridge. He met Lucia Santa Cruz, the stunning daughter of a former Chilean ambassador in Britain. Latin in temperament, very beautiful and feminine, but a clever historian with degrees from both London and Oxford universities, she was then the chief researcher on Lord Butler's memoirs at Cambridge.

Charles was completely fascinated by her for a time, but their friendship died. His family did not look with great enthusiasm on the young Prince becoming too deeply involved with a woman four years older than himself, and a foreigner to boot. Their romance ended, but she was one of the most significant women in his life.

According to friends from that university period, Charles 'discovered' girls at Cambridge. Following Lucia Santa Cruz, there was a long line of suitably British young ladies, all of whom had impeccable pedigrees. Among them were Lady Henrietta Fitzroy, eldest daughter of the Duke of Grafton, whose mother was Mistress of the Robes to the Queen; Lady Charlotte Manners, model-girl daughter of the Duke of Rutland; fellow Goon-humour lover Angela Nevill, whose parents Lord and Lady Rupert Nevill were close friends of the Queen; flaxen-haired Bettina Lindsay, offspring of the Tory politician Lord Balniel, and who favoured a beatnik life-style; a one-time firm favourite Georgina Russell, the elegantly beautiful daughter of British diplomat Sir John Russell—and of course, Lady Jane Wellesley.

For more than two years the pretty and petite only daughter of the most noble of families, the Duke and Duchess of Wellington, reigned supreme as the closest female companion of the Prince. They seemed so complete. She was always there waiting when he returned from the sea. Then, inexplicably, she suddenly faded from public view for about two years.

During the summer of 1977 however, Lady Jane Wellesley and Charles became close friends again, reviving speculation that she might become a royal bride. Also frequently at his side during 1977 was a friend from childhood, 22-year-old

Opposite: One of Charles' many
guests during Ascot Week
Right: A young African admirer
says a welcome with flowers

Lady Sarah Spencer, the daughter of Earl Spencer, an equerry to the Queen. Lady Sarah, whose step-grandmother is romantic novelist Barbara Cartland, accompanied the Prince to most of his polo engagements, and they often went off on solitary horserides together. They became closer when the Prince and his parents often spent weekends with Sarah and her family at their home in Northamptonshire.

While his friendship with Lady Jane cooled off for a couple of years, Charles turned to 26-year-old Caroline Longman, daughter of wealthy publisher Mark Longman. She was strikingly similar in appearance to Lady Jane and became a regular dinner and water-skiing companion. Her mother, Lady Elizabeth Longman, was a bridesmaid at the Queen's wedding in 1947.

A frequent companion also has been Fiona Watson, the beautiful daughter of Yorkshire landowner Lord Manton. She had a slightly more flamboyant side to her character, having once filled eleven pages of *Penthouse* magazine with pin-up pictures of herself. These are not quite the qualifications for future queenhood, but Charles found her fun to be with.

The lucky girl who does succeed in hooking what must be one of the biggest catches of the century will have a significant price to pay—the loss of her freedom.

From the time the engagement is announced she will have to bow completely to the wishes of her future in-laws. She will have to fit in with the life-style, manner and tastes of her fiancé's family.

Unlike most other brides, however, she will have no worries about the years ahead. A marriage bureau would describe the man she is about to walk with down the aisle of Westminster Abbey as having excellent prospects, to say the least.

His salary at the moment is £110,000 tax free, and the State would give the happy couple a huge wedding present of a massive boost in the Prince's allowances.

As Duke of Cornwall, Charles owns around 130,000 acres of some of the finest land in England with several thousand tenants, spread from Kennington Oval in South London to the Isles of Scilly. It is the profit from these estates that provides his allowances.

House hunting will be no problem. Prince Charles already has, waiting to be occupied, a giant love nest of eighty-three rooms surrounded by 3,000 of the loveliest acres in Kent. This is Chevening House, a seventeenth-century mansion donated to the nation by the seventh Earl of Stanhope, who died without an heir.

When, after their marriage, the young couple have friends down for the weekend, they will probably be able to squeeze them into one of ten enormous bedrooms, but they will have to ask them to share the five bathrooms.

It is one of the ironies of Charles' life that he has become a latter-day defender of the king that history has declared insane, George III.

George, long since known as the 'Mad King', reigned from 1770 to 1820. He was held responsible for, among many monarchial errors, the loss of the American colonies and a prolonged war with France. Writers, diarists and politicians of the day generally pronounced him to be a lunatic.

During one of his typical fits of pique he forced through Parliament a piece of legislation, which, more than 200 years later, is one of the major bonds in the strait-jacket that prevents Prince Charles from marrying whoever he wishes.

George was annoyed because two of his sons married commoners, so in 1772, he promulgated the Royal Marriage Act. Under this law 'no descendant of George II shall be capable of contracting matrimony without the previous consent of the king, and signified under the Great Seal, declared in Council and entered in the Privy Council books.'

In less formal language it means that Charles, as heir in direct line to Mad George's father, is in the hands of his mother and Parliament when it comes to picking a bride. He cannot simply take the girl round for tea one Sunday afternoon to meet the family. He has to satisfy the requirements of the Queen, the House of Lords and the House of Commons.

Until the age of twenty-five he could only marry with the consent of the Queen, but now, if she refuses permission, he can still ask for the approval of both Houses of Parliament. It seems highly unlikely however, even in this democratic age, that the Lords and the Commons would approve the match if the girl was so eminently unsuitable as to be formally rejected by Her Majesty.

George's parchment of marital mischief is just one of several archaic laws that hold in check Charles' rights as a suitor. The only regal legislation that does not seem to apply to him is the Statute of Treasons passed in 1351 which dwelled sternly on the chastity of ladies royal and promised the chopping block or gallows for any over-amorous seducer of princesses.

The greatest barriers to his freedom are the Acts governing not only the religion but the colour of his bride-to-be. Under an Act of 1689 she has to be a white Anglo-Saxon Protestant, so there would be just as big a fuss if he cast his eyes towards a Negress, an Arab or an Asian, as if he fell for a Roman Catholic.

This famous—or infamous—Bill of Rights also demands that Charles declare himself an 'enemy of the Catholic religion'. Needless to say it was passed at a time of great religious intolerance in England. However it still rules out very effectively any discussion on how a Roman Catholic could either change her religion, or merely agree to have the children brought up according to the teachings of the Church of England.

Unless this law is repealed during an era when both churches are drawing closer together, Charles must, after his coronation, speak out against the Roman Catholic doctrines of Transubstantiation, the Roman saints and the celebration of the mass.

To make the path of love even harder, this Act makes it quite clear that he would lose his crown if he marries a 'papist'. This threat to his throne is made still clearer in the Act of Succession of 1701—the law according to which Charles would be given the legal authority to rule. This Act invokes the out-dated Bill of Rights as the source of its insistence that he will forfeit his crown by marrying a Roman Catholic.

To enable Charles to have a Roman Catholic queen, Parliament would need to pass new laws either repealing the earlier Acts altogether or at least amending those passages which may be offensive to a large percentage of the non-protestant population of Britain and the Commonwealth.

There is a growing body of opinion within the Church of England which considers that the time has come to recognise that Henry VIII is dead and that the churches of Canterbury and Rome must be brought into the twentieth century. Charles, as king, would be the head of a Church of England, they say, that did not practise what it preached about the need for ecumenical links with other religions. There are others however, just as loyal to the Church of England, who feel otherwise, considering such ideas as too avant garde for the moment.

Hopes of changing such laws in the next few years certainly seem slim, when religious fervour is still so fiery among some of Charles' future subjects that they continue to fight a sectarian war in Ulster.

A future Queen who is Roman Catholic does, therefore, seem out of the question, unless Charles contemplates abdication. He takes the role of continuing the royal lineage of the House of Windsor so seriously however, and regards his own part in the destiny of his family so highly, that abandoning the throne for love does not seem in tune with his character.

If he so drastically followed the example of his great-uncle, the Duke of Windsor, and put love before the throne it would probably bring into question the British monarchy altogether. Would two abdications in forty years be too much for the British people to swallow?

Because of the very responsible attitude he has towards his duties as heir, all the speculation during 1977 about a betrothal to 23-year-old

(Continued on page 63)

59

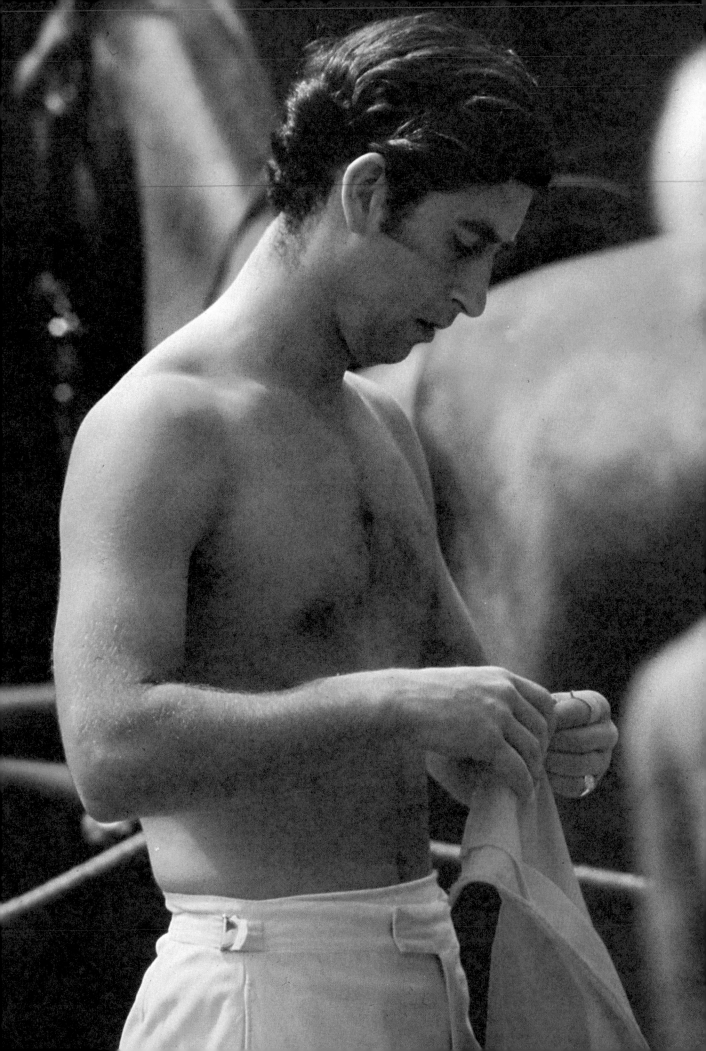

Roman Catholic Princess Marie-Astrid of Luxembourg eventually angered him, although he has always before taken an amused view of speculation on his marriage prospects. Every few months a new name keeps popping up in the world's gossip columns, some of them girls he has been genuinely fond of, but many he hardly knows at all.

He greets most of this speculation with wry amusement and when the gossip about his love-life gets a little out of hand he takes it in his stride. He once shrugged his shoulders and said, in the manner of a much slandered film star:'The time to get anxious, in a way, is when nobody's interested at all.'

The 'Astrid Affair', as it became known at Buckingham Palace, was too much however, and it raised his hackles in a most untypical way. One reason was that he had never even contemplated marrying her. He had met Marie-Astrid on only three occasions and he could not remember these clearly. She was merely one of the thousands he had shaken hands with in official line-ups. Out of curiosity he traced the first time she was introduced to him—at the age of fifteen, she attended Charles' investiture as Prince of Wales in 1969.

Despite this, gossip columnists at home and abroad persisted in linking pretty, fair-haired 'Asty', as she became known, with Charles.

Had not the Queen and Prince Philip visited her father and mother the Grand Duke and Grand Duchess in Luxembourg? Then the Grand Duke came over to Sandringham to shoot with Prince Philip. The Grand Duke was, after all, educated at Britain's leading Roman Catholic public school, Ampleforth, in Yorkshire. During the Second World War he became a private in the Irish Guards, carrying out sentry duties at Buckingham Palace. Surely he qualified as the perfect father of a future queen of the United Kingdom?

Charles himself had said:'The one advantage of marrying a princess, for instance, or somebody from a royal family, is that they know what happens.' Significant?

Then Marie-Astrid went to Cambridge to take an English language course. More significant? She was also a direct descendant of Charles I—surely this made her almost an ersatz Englishwoman?

Even talks between Roman Catholic and Church of England representatives over the sticky matter of religious difficulties were reported to have taken place. Experts on the delicate subtleties of royal accession were roped in to give their opinion that Astrid need not renounce her Catholicism. Girl children of the marriage could remain attached to Rome while boys could satisfy the Church of England by supporting Canterbury.

Should girls only be the result of the proposed 'union' then the line of succession could pass to Charles' younger brother Prince Andrew, hopefully provided with a spouse who was a fine, upstanding Protestant.

Despite denials from Buckingham Palace about any romance, the rumour continued. The *Daily Express* was particularly doubtful of royal denials. It had crossed swords with the palace on this very aspect of royal public relations at least twice . . . when it reported exclusively that Princess Anne and Mark Phillips were to marry, and when it beat the rest of Fleet Street with the sad news that Princess Margaret and Lord Snowdon were breaking up.

The same high-up source who had provided these scoops also leaked to the *Express* that Charles and Marie-Astrid were to announce their engagement on Monday, 20 June 1977. When this authoritative newspaper published the news a few days in advance it seemed to confirm all the rumours in the gossip columns.

Charles and most of the Royal Family were confronted with the revelation over breakfast at Windsor Castle, where they were staying during the Queen's Silver Jubilee celebrations. One of the royal dukes chided Charles: 'I see you've got yourself engaged at last, Wales.'

The Prince enjoyed the family leg-pulling for a while, but then he lost his sense of humour. He felt a touch of anger and ordered the Queen's Press Secretary, Ronald Allison, to put out an official denial. He also instructed that this had to be a personal turn-down, direct from himself.

Allison later told the authors of this book that not only was there no intention of marriage to Marie-Astrid, either then or in the foreseeable future, but that Prince Charles was not due to become engaged to anyone at that time; as far as Allison knew, the Prince had not met the right girl yet.

'Mind you,' added the palace spokesman, 'who can predict? He might fall in love with someone between now and the end of the year. No one can say.'

In fairness to newspapers, it should be pointed out that Charles seems to enjoy keeping everyone guessing, turning up in public with a rich variety of attractive young aristocratic ladies. During the week of the 'engagement' announcement he had set noble tongues wagging by being seen in the company of two perfectly eligible young ladies: Lady Camilla Fane, daughter of the Earl of Westmorland, and Lady Sarah Spencer.

Having a string of girlfriends would not be unusual for any other eligible bachelor, but with Charles every one of them is brought into the national queen-spotting game. He admits that occasionally he looks at one of his regular companions and asks himself: 'I wonder if I could ever marry her?'

63

(Continued on page 67)

Charles in congenial company at the Tradewinds Hotel, Suva

An intimate moment between Charles and Lady Sarah

He has always insisted that he would not get married until he was around thirty, 'after one has seen a great deal of life, met a large number of girls, fallen in love now and then, and knows what it's all about.'

His sound, sane approach to love is worthy of inclusion in a marriage-guidance pamphlet: 'I feel an awful lot of people have got the wrong idea of what love is all about. I think it is rather more than just falling madly in love with somebody and having a love affair for the rest of your married life.

'I think it's much more than that. It's basically a very strong friendship. As often as not you have interests and ideas in common and also a great deal of affection. I think you are very lucky if you find the person attractive in the physical *and* the mental sense.

'In many cases you fall madly ''in love'' with somebody with whom you are really infatuated rather than in love. To me marriage, which may be for fifty years, seems to be one of the biggest and most responsible steps to be taken in one's life.'

Charles knows full well that his position is vastly different from that of his sister. Anne could marry a commoner because she is not immediate heir to the throne. He is in a unique position. He can consider a commoner, but the regal traditions he must continue make such a choice very difficult for him.

Although princesses are trained to do the job he has in mind for a wife, as Charles has said, it still looks most unlikely that he will make his choice from a palace. The girl who will be the next Queen is probably going to come from one of Britain's stately homes.

Suitable princesses are thin on the ermine-shaded ground, but there is an abundance of candidates, as he has happily found, in the smart town houses of Belgravia and the affluent halls in the shires.

On one of the many occasions when he has been asked about the girl he would marry, the Prince answered: 'This is awfully difficult because you have to remember that when you marry in my position you are going to marry someone who perhaps one day is going to be Queen.

'I've got to choose somebody very carefully, I think, who could fill this particular role and it has got to be somebody pretty special. I often feel I would like to marry somebody English or perhaps Welsh. Well, British anyway.'

The age of the arranged marriage has passed. Such is the affection among the British people for their Royal Family that his future subjects would want Charles to marry a woman he truly loved, who would give him the strength of a happy home life and support him with her affection while he carries out one of the most difficult tasks in the twentieth century.

Charles on tour doing a love dance with a girl from the Cook Islands and *(overleaf)* a conga dance at the Yacht Club in Fiji

Walt Disney's most extravagant scriptwriter could never have created such a fairy-tale scene—a queen in a golden coach pulled by six white horses, a handsome prince in dashing uniform riding behind her, and the sun coming through the clouds just in time for the triumphal procession through the cheering masses. Yet this happened in London on the memorable 7 June 1977, as part of the Silver Jubilee celebrations marking the twenty-fifth anniversary of the Queen's accession to the throne.

Military bands and thousands of troops lined the two-mile route from Buckingham Palace to St Paul's cathedral. Hundreds of thousands of rain-soaked flagwavers from all over the world had hardly enough space to breathe, let alone cheer and shout, as they crammed the pavements.

At the head of this procession to the thanksgiving service in the cathedral was a troop of the scarlet-clad Royal Canadian Mounted Police. Behind them were landaus and glass coaches, carrying generals, admirals and air marshals.

The Queen, with the Duke of Edinburgh sitting beside her, waved to the crowds through the windows of the 216-year-old Golden State Coach. Riding in a place of honour just behind the right wheel was Prince Charles.

He was mounted on a sleek black horse just given to him by the Mounties. With a silver sword at his side, he was dressed in the tall bearskin and crimson jacket of a colonel in the Welsh Guards. Across his chest was a lavish display of decorations. In truth, a suitable escort for a queen.

That he was posted in pride of place near to his parents, seemed to signify the ever-increasing official role he now has in royal life. He is gradually taking from his parents much of the burden of public appearances and world tours. He is getting more deeply involved in the responsibility of preserving the crown and running the nation.

The Prince, like other members of the Royal Family, has had doubts about the desire of his mother's subjects for the monarchial system to continue. This response to the Jubilee from young and old dispelled his worries.

Most of the crowd were teenagers and young men and women in their early twenties, the very people with whom he has always tried so hard to communicate. Some wore tatty jeans and had long unruly hair, but they demonstrated their love for the monarchy with their shouts, flag waving and football-style banners proclaiming slogans such as 'The Queen Rules, OK!'

Charles soaked in every second of it all as he rode behind his mother and father. Talking about that day later, he commented: 'It was great fun and, when done well and tastefully, there's nothing more marvellous than this sort of thing. Judging by the number of people on the streets,

and their enthusiasm, they enjoyed it too. Apart from anything else it was the most wonderful expression of happiness and affection for the Queen.'

It also had its droll moment for Charles. He nearly fell off his horse at St Paul's because someone had put the dismounting block under the horse instead of alongside it. 'When I saw it later on television it wasn't as disastrous as I had thought.'

His formal title is His Royal Highness the Prince Charles Philip Arthur George, Prince of Wales and Earl of Chester, Duke of Cornwall and Rothesay, Earl of Carrick and Baron of Renfrew, Lord of the Isles and Great Steward of Scotland, Knight of the Garter.

The Prince of Wales and Earl of Chester are joint titles most closely associated with a male heir apparent of a reigning monarch. They go back to Edward II who had them conferred on him in February 1301. On the death of a Prince of Wales and Earl of Chester in the lifetime of a sovereign, the titles do not pass on to the current holder's son. They must be recreated with each reign.

Cornwall and the five Scottish titles came by tradition to Charles, as eldest son of the sovereign, from the moment the Queen ascended to the throne. Edward III created his son the Duke of Cornwall in March 1337, making it clear that the title should descend to the eldest sons of the kings and queens of England forever.

The Scottish titles go back to the fourteenth century. They were brought to England when James VI of Scotland became James I of England after the death of the first Queen Elizabeth. Charles is now the holder of them as heir to the old kingdom of Scotland.

The Queen made Charles a Knight of the Garter when he was ten years old, but he was not invested and installed in the Royal Chapel at Windsor until 1968, when he reached the age of twenty.

One of his first formal steps towards the eventual responsibility of the throne was in the autumn of 1972 when, at the age of twenty-three, he was appointed a Councillor of State—together with the Queen Mother—to handle the official affairs of the realm while the Queen visited Australia.

This function is vital to the running of Britain and the Commonwealth because, constitutionally, the works of governments at home and abroad have to be officially approved by the sovereign or her properly appointed representatives.

Charles embarked on his first solo royal tour soon after he came down from Cambridge in 1970, when he went off on a 25,000 mile round-trip to Fiji and New Zealand. This seemed to set the pattern for all his future public appearances. He asked for as much informality as possible, taking

75

(Continued on page 79)

Opposite: Trying the traditional Fijian drink, Yagona
Previous page: The 'Blackfoot chief' in Canada

Polo as a Commonwealth link — with
fellow players after a game in Accra

the wind out of official stuffiness.

He likes people to approach him. This is his style. 'Yet,' he says, 'many people are too shy and overcome in the presence of royalty. Only the dignitaries seem to talk to me on well-tried subjects, usually of little interest.'

He understands the difficulties of breaking down the barriers: 'Unfortunately the nicest people are those who won't come up and make themselves known. They're terrified of being seen to be friendly in case they'll be accused of sucking up to me and because they imagine, quite wrongly, that I won't want to talk to them.

'I used to think "Good God, what's wrong? Do I smell? Have I forgotten to change my socks?" I realise now that I have to make a bit of the running and show that I am a reasonable human being. An awful lot of people say eventually: "Good Lord, you're not nearly as pompous as I thought you were going to be." '

Charles has become a fully paid-up member of the most efficient team of national drum-beaters in the world. The Queen and Prince Philip and now the Prince are the salesmen of British exports. Wherever they go, they help to improve British trade with a subtle soft-sell that other industrial nations cannot match. A West German diplomat said at a reception during the State visit to Japan: 'It's quite fantastic the effect the Royal Family has on bringing prestige to exports—it's unfair competition to the rest of us.'

Charles is also helping to keep the Commonwealth idea of unity alive, showing how the throne can still act as the imperial lynch-pin. This is especially important now, when there is talk of cutting ties with Britain in Australia and calls for separatism in Canada.

What often appears an informal, freebooting trip on the surface is in fact meticulously planned ahead. Before a visit an advance party goes over a route with a stopwatch, timing every expected pause, allowing the odd minute for the Prince suddenly spending more time with someone, or at some interesting place. The same party also arranges for hospitals and surgeons to be alerted en route in case of an accident, and his medical records are sent ahead.

Those likely to meet him are advised on the protocol of shaking hands. 'Do not put out your hand unless the Prince puts out his hand first. If he offers you his hand, take it. But do not shake it. The Prince does the shaking.'

The travelling entourage of the Prince is usually made up of his private secretary, Squadron Leader David Checketts, a press secretary, an equerry, an air attache (if he's going by air), at least one armed personal detective, a secretary to his private secretary and a valet.

They make up a travelling boardroom. It is like the chairman of a company taking his top men 79

Charles when he was made a tribal chief in Ghana

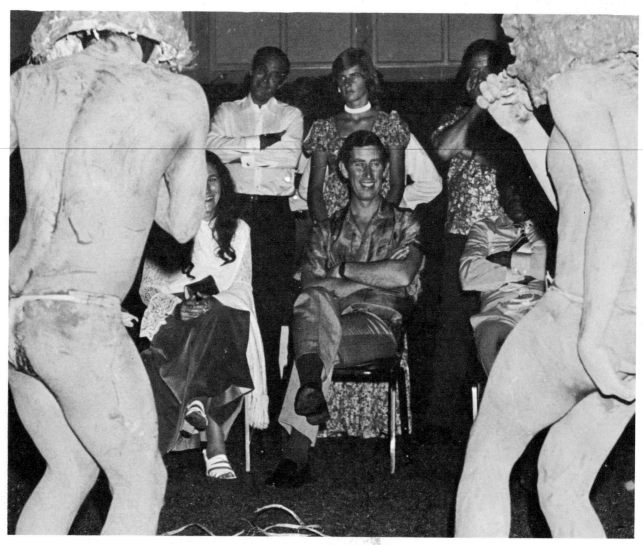

Watching a mock attack by the Mudmen of Papua New Guinea

and aides with him, working as they jet along.

He has two regular detectives, chosen from the London Metropolitan Police, who have been with him for a number of years. They take it in turn to protect the Prince, and travel with him at all times.

He has great energy for work and usually gets through the programme of the day with the precision of a Swiss watch. He sets a rigorous pace. In Canberra, he once roused everyone at 5.30 am to go swimming sixty miles away by car. At 10 am the same morning, he was back in the Australian capital ready to start with the first official engagement.

While on tour, Charles often stays up until 2 am, researching on what to expect the next day, and on the people he is likely to meet. He does this thoroughly and often surprises someone with well-informed questions about their past that appear to be off the cuff.

He rehearses speeches with care and allows for passages where he expects people to laugh. When he stands in front of the microphone he is word perfect.

Out of courtesy to her position, he never refers to 'my mother' in a speech, always to 'the Queen'. He is usually more informal as far as Prince Philip is concerned and frequently calls him 'my father'.

If there is an official programme he does not like it to be altered—unless it is his decision. Calls for impromptu speeches, or switches in arrangements made without warning by local officials, do not please him.

In Tasmania during an Australian visit, one of the organisers at an agricultural fair asked him to say a few words. This was not part of the schedule, but he could hardly appear churlish when he was asked so publicly over the loudspeaker system to address the crowd. He had no previous briefing to give him material for a speech, but he said a few cheerful, harmless sentences. He was annoyed though, and, seemingly as a punishment to the organisers, he walked so rapidly round the exhibits that all the officials could hardly keep up with him, never slowing down to take his usual interest in what was going on.

He does not like to be abused. If there is a programme he will stick to it, and he expects others to do their part properly.

As he flies round his mother's world-wide kingdom, Charles is very wary about getting involved in local politics. Before a visit, the advance party or the local embassy assesses any sticky problems he might face.

He gets a run-down on the topics to keep clear of and any person to be on his guard against. Despite this need for the crown to be seen to be absolutely impartial, some local bigwig is often tempted to rope Charles in to help him with a bit of electoral perfidy.

It might be blatant exploitation of a royal visit so that the Prince calls to see only those buildings and enterprises accredited to one particular party, or the proposed tour may be restricted to areas where voters traditionally favour one political colour. A speech of welcome may become an excuse to add the partisan flavour of the hustings. At such moments Charles may show his displeasure on the platform, or pass it on to the gentleman concerned later.

He found an amusing way of facing up to an unavoidable involvement in local politics when he flew from Darwin in Northern Australia to Papua New Guinea late in 1975.

He went there to hand over constitutional documents from the Queen, cutting the territory's last colonial links and granting independence. While the several hundred small tribes carried on their interminable wars in the 15,000 feet high mountains, down in the main towns the politicians were at each other's throats. For two years this lush area, still unexploited in parts, had governed itself under the watchful eye of Australia. Now it was to get complete independence, and the local leaders were squabbling. One of the islands rich in copper, Bourgainville, threatened to break away from the new nation.

Charles took the unusual step of turning to the Bible for chastening words of advice for the quarrelling politicians. At a service in the Roman Catholic cathedral at Port Moresby, the capital, he quoted St Paul's epistle to the Romans: 'Everyone must obey the State authorities, for no authority exists without God's permission, and the existing authorities have been put there by God.

'Whoever opposes the existing authority opposes what God has ordered and anyone who does so will bring judgement on himself.' It was a brave and original try—but the arguments still continued.

No matter where he is in the world, Charles has to keep up with bags of duty mail that are flown in regularly. His staff help by sorting them out into readily understood batches. There is a pile for official letters of State, another for personal letters, and one for the enormous number of requests for him to lend his support to a charity or business scheme, while yet another basket contains just friendly, hand-written greetings from unknown, ordinary folk, who want to send him a few cheery words of encouragement.

Charles sends his replies, like all the members of the Royal Family, on special thick paper called 'Original Turkey Mill Kent'. If it is a personal letter he often handwrites it himself, but usually one of the secretaries who travel with him types his answers. They bear no stamp, but are marked with the letters ER, the royal insignia, on the front and back.

On public occasions Charles always tries to show interest, no matter how often he may have seen similar fancy footwork in countless halls and arenas and heard so many conventional orations.

He stays bright, alert, and inquisitive for two reasons. One is that questing spirit to know about everyone and everything, while the other is the natural development of his royal training. A close friend of the royal household said of this aspect of Charles' life: 'If you've been brought up to feel it's your duty to be interested in everything and everybody, after a while it's second nature to you.'

A visit to Canada in the summer of 1977 was typical of what a strain on stamina and patience a royal visit can be. Charles left London early one Tuesday morning on an eight-hour flight to Calgary in Alberta, the site of that world famous rodeo, the Stampede.

Because of time differences, the Prince had already added an extra five hours to his working day when he stepped off the Air Canada jumbo jet. It was only eleven o'clock in the morning in the Prairie capital, while back in London it was time for tea.

Most of his fellow passengers went off to relax in hotel rooms and recover from the journey, but Charles began a nine-hour working day starting with a smiling, hand-waving parade through town. He took in lunch with some of the local worthies followed by a cocktail party for 200 journalists covering the tour, and another round of formal glad-handing before making his weary way to bed.

Early next morning he flew by helicopter to a remote stretch of territory deep in Indian country where he showed his usual interest in the goings on of exotically named people such as Chief Nelson Small Legs Junior, Chief Pretty Youngman, Chief Him Shot Both Sides, and 3,000 other assorted Blackfoot representatives.

He moved in and out of tepees paying the expected royal attention to a lecture on the art of constructing these mobile homes. For the benefit of television cameras he mounted a horse and trotted for a hundred yards. The pipe of peace, which did not give out any smoke for the Prince, was handed round; then Charles sat cross-legged on the ground while he listened to two hours of long speeches by the chiefs.

In pouring rain he carried out a tour of more tepees then, dripping wet but still smiling, he dashed into the shelter of a large marquee for an hour of traditional tribal dancing. Scores of colourfully dressed Indians circled slowly, stamping their feet to the beat of tom-toms—the sort of scene most people see for just a few minutes in a Western film prior to the warriors riding away to eliminate General Custer and his men.

To lovers of native customs the thud of the drums and low moans of the dancers must have been very exciting. It takes a special brand of stoicism, however, to look interested and ask intelligent questions when you are soaked to the skin.

The highlight of the third day was when the royal visitor donned buckskins and a long feathered headdress, was daubed with yellow greasepaint and dubbed HRH Red Crow, an honorary chief. Charles enjoyed the fun of it all.

On the fourth day, looking very tired, Charles changed from indian to cowboy. Wearing a wide-brimmed stetson, cattleman's boots, and a smartly-tailored western suit, he mounted a bronco and led the five-mile-long procession that opened the Stampede. He was joined by his younger brother Andrew, who was spending a year at school in Canada. As he was pushed, shoved and shouted at among the crowds at the rodeo, Charles seemed relieved to have at least one familiar face beside him.

At the end of almost a week of smiling, waving, rain-sodden dashing about, speech-making, hand-shaking, and being pleasant to thousands of strangers, Charles went to bed exhausted. An American reporter, used to seeing his own President take on such a daily workload at election times only, commented: 'That guy works so hard you'd think he was running for office.'

As a prince on royal duties, Charles does his utmost to please people, and make them feel at ease, while at the same time preserving the dignity of his office. Sometimes this causes him personal discomfort. During that visit to Papua New Guinea he was forced at all times to wear uniform; this was requested by the Government because, it was explained to him, that if he was not in uniform the tribesmen would not recognise him as a great chief. Considering that the temperatures were shatteringly high, his discomfort is easily imagined.

On the island of Bau in Fiji, he watched a two-hour display of tribal war dances. Unaware that the Prince was not as used to the oven-heat as themselves, the local chiefs had given him a seat facing the strong sun. He was soon extremely uncomfortable and had to fight against falling into a torpor, so great was the heat. His lips were bone-dry but he never said a word. At last one of his hosts noticed his obvious discomfort but unwittingly added to it by giving him a strange-

(Continued on page 86)

83

Attending ceremonies with Ashanti chiefs in Accra

Some of Prince Charles' fan-club waiting
for him to arrive in Abidjan

tasting drink made out of grass roots crushed to a powder and mixed with water.

Despite the sour smell, Charles gulped the drink back, though from the grimace on his face it was clear that this beverage would never figure on a list of his favourite drinks. He has often said that his stomach can take anything. On this occasion he proved it.

Preserving the Commonwealth is one of Charles' great aims in life. He likes to think there is a family spirit about it, where everyone feels they know each other, and that they have something in common. This is based, he believes, on a common language, culture, experience and history.

He has pointed out on more than one occasion that the Queen is no longer just the Queen of England. Thanks to several Acts of Parliament in Australia, Canada and New Zealand, she is just as much owned as Queen by these nations as she is by Great Britain.

This was the point he tried to make when he gave a confusing answer to a question during the July 1977 Commonwealth Youth Conference. In an off-the-cuff reply he said: 'I don't think it would be a disaster if Britain withdrew from the Commonwealth and I am sure it could survive without Britain.'

He was saying this to try to show the strength of the Commonwealth as he sees it. He also said: 'I believe that the Queen, as head of the Commonwealth, plays an important part in keeping the whole thing together.

'It is a wider family than it was and it is the Commonwealth and not the British Commonwealth. Too often people are inclined to treat the concept of the Commonwealth with cynicism, or to reject it altogether as an anachronism and complete waste of everybody's time and effort.'

Two hundred young Commonwealth delegates gathered in London from forty-five countries, were given a clear indication too about how Charles pins his hopes on them: 'Above all I believe it is up to the young of the Commonwealth to show that they believe that association has something to offer the modern world, because without your support, interest and encouragement, it will only be a matter of time before the whole thing fades away through lack of interest.'

He sets himself the task of trying to break through differences of colour and race, political systems, language and wealth in order to keep together what is still one of the liveliest international alliances in the world. He attempts to link black and white, mud hut with penthouse suite, the universal have-nots with the haves.

Charles was given one of the greatest welcomes he has ever experienced on his travels

(Continued on page 90)

In Alberta during that tough tour of Canada

86

The Prince meets the people of Port Moresby, Papua New Guinea

abroad in Abidjan on the Ivory Coast in the spring of 1977. On the day of his arrival a million people lined the eight-mile route from the airport to the presidential palace.

It took more than an hour to cover that short distance. Makeshift bands used old oil drums and pots and pans to hammer out a noisy African rhythm. Women sported blue and red dresses with pictures of the Prince printed on them. Teenage girls and boys danced and weaved around the royal car.

On this same tour of West Africa there was a moment when the Andover of the Queen's Flight, carrying the royal party, had to suddenly zoom away from danger as it was about to land at a small airfield in northern Ghana.

After the RAF captain of the aircraft had been given permission to land by the control tower, the commander of the guard of honour ordered his men to get into position. To do so he marched them across the runway—in the path of the approaching plane. The pilot sharply boosted his power, pulled back the control column and roared above the heads of the startled troops to circuit again for another landing a few minutes later.

Charles then walked down the aircraft steps with a wry smile and ignored the obvious embarrassment of the unfortunate officer in charge, as he was invited to inspect the troops he had very nearly ploughed through.

The main event of his visit to Ghana was a gathering of dozens of Ashanti tribal chiefs at a durbar in Kumasi. These descendants of the fierce warriors who fought a series of bloody battles against the British crown in the nineteenth century, rarely gather in such numbers except to honour a high ranking visitor.

Hundreds of the chiefs' followers came with them and there was a lively parade in front of Charles lasting more than an hour. The weather was of the same torrid nature that used to drive white men to early graves. To ease the burden for the Prince and his party, cool drinks and beer were kept at the back of the dais in ice-boxes.

Outdoor life suits Prince Charles extremely well, and this explains why he has so much love for Australia. He feels he became a man there and that he will always remember those beautiful days spent in the bush while at his Australian school. This experience may explain why he is not frightened to speak his mind and why he feels that he should be seen for what he is, warts and all, not as the product of image makers.

'Images are dangerous things to cultivate because most people can see through any artificial character,' he has said, adding in one of his jocular moods: 'I suppose in some circles I could improve my image by growing my hair to a more fashionable length, being seen regularly at the Playboy Club and dressing in excrutiatingly tight clothes. This would, however, give my tailor apoplexy!'

He told a group of students in Ottawa: 'The best compliment I like to hear is when people say about me "Oh, he's so ordinary." The most important thing for me is to have concern for people, to show it and provide some form of leadership.' His concern for people was evident in his maiden speech as a member of the House of Lords in June 1974. He called for wider education, more parks and recreational facilities, for a general awakening to 'the challenge of removing the dead hand of boredom from mankind.'

He pursued this theme more than a year later in his second speech in the chamber, when he called for more facilities for the youth of Britain. He is sensitive to the problems of young people and would like to see more organisations created to channel energy away from street or soccer stadium violence into community help services.

Charles' interest in the social conditions of modern life, his awareness of community problems and concern for the well-being of the nation have been demonstrated in his work for Wales.

When the Queen and Prince Philip decided the time had come for Charles to take up the title of Prince of Wales, they were determined that, unlike the late Duke of Windsor, who bore that title, their son should develop more than just a nodding acquaintance with the place. He was to learn the Welsh language and culture, to prove wrong all the jibes of Welsh nationalism against 'Carlo' as one cynical song called him.

When he went to the University College of Wales, Aberystwyth, to absorb some 'Welshness' there was not exactly a welcome in every hillside: in some of the mountains the Free Wales Army even had their bombs ready.

The Welsh language, rich and poetic, is not one of the easiest to learn and is spoken by less than half of the population in fact. Yet in a few months at Aberystwyth Charles mastered enough phrases and grammar not only to give his investiture speech in Welsh but to hold a reasonably fluent conversation in the tongue. He was the first English prince to speak and understand Welsh.

To add to his cultural knowledge of Wales he delved into the abundant, romantic Welsh literature which has an unbroken literary history going back to the sixth century. He worked hard to understand the country and its people and at last even the most ardent nationalist tipped his hat in admiration.

By the time he was invested with the title by the Queen at Caernarvon Castle on 1 July 1969, an opinion poll showed that ninety per cent of the Welsh were in favour of the ceremony. They felt it 91 was an honour Wales had waited too long to receive.

Charles recognised that part of the resentment against him was due to the opinion of many Welshmen that, over the centuries, the English-dominated Parliament at Westminster had ignored their needs and problems. Leading hard lives as miners, hill farmers or fishermen, many had become angry or hurt, thinking they were neglected by London.

This is one of the reasons why the Prince has committed himself with such enthusiasm to Welsh affairs, hoping he can make up for what so many of his subjects regard as centuries of apathy.

Unlike most of his predecessors, the current Prince of Wales devotes a large part of his time to the principality and its affairs. Be it Welsh industry, art, music or the almost religious national rite of rugby, he tries to get involved.

When he is in the valleys and mountains on one of his grass-roots tours of the area, he often pops into a pub or calls in on that most masculine of Welsh institutions, the rugby club bar.

On one occasion he walked without warning into The Buck public house at Newtown in Wales and then, in the parlance of today, 'chatted up' the attractive barmaid. Charles bought friendly, blonde 22-year-old Lynda Gwilt a gin and tonic while he talked with her.

Another day he joined in a beer-swilling sing-song with the unusually named Gilfach Goch rugby club in Glamorgan. He was in the area for the far more serious purpose of presenting the town with a Prince of Wales conservation award for a land reclamation scheme, but he fancied the idea of finishing his visit by having a pint with the boys.

At the other end of royal involvement are the many hours of work he puts in for Welsh industry and the preservation of the countryside.

He has developed a hearty affection for the country, and is anxious to preserve its beauty. He is Chairman of the Welsh Countryside Committee, and some of the methods he advocates to protect nature might seem rather revolutionary for a prince. He advised members of his committee to organise protest demonstrations outside any factories that might be polluting his beloved countryside.

He told them: 'The aim is to create awareness that efforts in conservation and pollution control are designed for the long-term good of this country. To go on virtually destroying what we live in until the final horror really strikes us and then try to do something is surely an insult to human rational thinking.'

He also called on the trade unions to use their power to persuade management to stop pollution.

As Chairman of the Countryside Committee he has urged local councils in the principality to try to improve rural roads without damaging the beauty of the river-etched hills and valleys. Never one to mince his words over something he has a passion for, he described the motor car as the 'most destructive plaything the world has ever known'. Its survival depended on acres of concrete and macadam, he claimed, and, unlike its forerunners, it could not adapt to a new 'ecological niche', even if it could find one.

In a challenge to the motor and civil engineering industries he said: 'Society committed to a machine that requires tracks to be scoured across the increasingly precious countryside can either shrug its shoulders and excuse unoriginal and unimaginative road-building or press for designs which harmonise as far as possible with the natural features of the countryside.'

He tries to rally support for his cause with such rousing cries to the Welsh as: 'I want to see as many people as possible in Wales show that they love their country as much as they say and sing they do.' Generally, they have responded to his call.

Schoolchildren, local authorities, village groups and individuals have busied themselves with projects to improve the quality of life. The countryside is being cleared of rubbish, recreational facilities improved, wild flowers and trees preserved, dirty rivers cleaned and ancient monuments restored.

Demonstrating how his interest is not merely in flowers, rivers and trees, he has also brought more industry to Wales. In Japan he met the shrewd, tough president of the Sony Corporation, Mr Akio Morita, on a visit to Expo 70 at Osaka. Mr Morita mentioned that his company planned to build their first plant in Europe, and Charles persuaded him to think of Wales. His efforts paid off and two years later the Prince flew straight from his passing out parade as a helicopter pilot at Yeovilton to open the new Sony factory at Bridgend, which produces colour television sets.

His involvement in all things Welsh includes being Colonel of the Welsh Guards, the youngest regiment of the Brigade of Guards. It is in their uniform that he rides with his mother every June to take part in that most spectacular ceremony of Trooping the Colour, on Horse Guards Parade in London.

He first donned the white-plumed bearskin and scarlet jacket for the celebration of the sovereign's birthday while he was in the Royal Navy in 1975. Since then, and for the future, it has become one of the most important yearly engagements in his diary.

This mounting involvement in public events has brought the heir to the throne closer to millions of people on a global scale. He feels nothing is too much trouble if it helps him to establish a link with those he will rule.

The new Knight of the Garter with his grandmother

Chapter 7
Prince Charles Limited

When the global cheers have faded, and the last hand has been shaken, Charles still has work to do to earn his royal wages.

Part of the strange nature of his role is that he does not get paid by either the nation or the Commonwealth, for being the heir apparent. He must take on extra work to raise the money—a kind of blue-blooded moonlighting.

Putting a price on junior kingship is something that cannot be negotiated by trade union leaders. There are no provisions in any known agreements on conditions of employment.

Such are the arrangements in his case, though, that Charles' annual salary does not cost the British taxpayer a penny. In fact he pays taxes himself. To earn enough money to carry out his duties, pay his living expenses, cover the costs of his staff, his clothes and uniforms, his sports car, his polo ponies, his entertaining and his weekends away, Charles runs a complex but profitable business, which makes a gross profit annually of more than two million pounds.

The main source of income is the Duchy of Cornwall, a rich property and landowning enterprise west of London. He supplements this with other personal investments.

Charles does not pay any regular tax on his income from the Duchy but the usual percentage goes to the Chancellor of the Exchequer from earnings in other fields. Like many in his family, including the Queen, he has private investments that bring him an unknown—but not immodest—return. He has to fill in a tax form every year for these profits, just like any ordinary citizen.

The Royal Family's shareholding operations are dealt with for them by three 'blue chip' stockbrokers in the City of London, who receive their instructions from the long-established regal bankers, Coutts & Co. Such are the efforts made to ensure that Charles, as well as his relations, does not have an opportunity to make use of privileged information which could affect the market, that he rarely knows which stock he is holding.

Coutts act as the first barrier to his knowledge of how his money is invested; then the three royal stockbrokers have discretionary powers to act as they please, without even telling the bankers in which companies the Prince has stockholdings.

Unlike other leading members of the Royal Family, he does not receive any support through what is known as the Civil List. This is the system Parliament uses to pay the Queen and others close to her.

Most of the profit from the Duchy of Cornwall is ploughed back into administering and improving the estates. Depending on the yearly outlay, the average net profits are £220,000. Half of this is given to the nation while Charles holds on to the remainder as his annual pay packet.

The rate for the job then, is £110,000 tax free. It has been estimated that at current rates of taxation he would have to earn a gross of a million pounds a year to be able to put that net figure in the bank. It still leaves him earning nearly twice as much as his father.

The annual Civil List pay for other members of the Royal Family is £1,900,000 for the Queen (plus an estimated £300,000 from her Duchy of Lancaster estates); Prince Philip £85,000; Princess Anne £50,000 (increased from £15,000 after her marriage); Princess Margaret £55,000; and the Queen Mother £155,000. The £100,000 or so that Charles takes from the Duchy is conservative when compared to what the jolly, Paris-loving Prince of Wales of a hundred years ago pocketed as his personal income. Edward, who did not reach the throne until the turn of the century, had a personal income from the Duchy of £50,000 a year. Allowing for inflation, this sum would be in the millionaire class today.

Charles decided to come to this arrangement with the Government on his twenty-first birthday. Until then nearly all the income from the Duchy of Cornwall went to the Chancellor of the Exchequer. The Queen was given £15,000 to look after the needs of her son up to the age of eighteen and then she received £30,000, all from the royal lands to the West.

The total area of the Duchy is 130,000 acres, which makes Charles one of the biggest landowners in Britain. It is a mixture of farms and country homesteads, old terraced houses, shops and at least one pub in London.

Its interests are spread over Cornwall, Devon, Somerset, Dorset, Gloucestershire and Wiltshire as well as all the Isles of Scilly. There are 850 tenants in the area of Kennington in South London, and thousands more elsewhere.

If Charles visits the famous Oval cricket ground in Kennington to see a Test Match, it is also a case of the landlord paying a call since he owns that green turf as well. Not much further than it would take a batsman to whack a ball there is Lambeth Walk, made famous by the old Cockney song. This too belongs to the Prince. Kennington was originally known as 'Kings Town', marking the association with centuries of Dukes of Cornwall.

Outside London his tenants include sheep farmers on Dartmoor, Cornish tin miners, and daffodil growers in the Scillies. He also owns the site of the notorious Dartmoor Prison.

On the river Helford in Cornwall he has an oyster farm which produces a million succulent morsels every year, selling at around £2 or £3 a dozen. Recently he subcontracted this operation to the giant British marketing company of MacFisheries.

Apart from having land on which hundreds of farmers are his tenants, Charles also has a 550 acre farm of his own. This is Duchy Home Farm at Stoke Climsland in East Cornwall, which breeds high quality beef cattle called Devon Red Rubies. He takes a very active interest in running the place and helps Britain's exports by selling some of his 300-strong herd to foreign breeders.

One of the odd perks is that any whale or porpoise washed ashore and stranded off the beaches of Cornwall belongs to Charles by ancient right. In the Scilly Isles the annual dues used to be 300 puffins, but these have now been reduced to fifty. He is still waiting to receive them.

The estates, together with the title, date back to the early fourteenth century when Edward III created the title in 1337 and began the tradition of passing it down through history as both an honour and a source of income for the eldest sons of monarchs.

It is the oldest of such honours in nobility, because until Edward III chose it for his 6-year-old son, Edward the Black Prince, the word 'duke' did not exist in Britain. It comes from the Latin 'dux' meaning leader.

King Edward's charter instituting the dukedom is still preserved in barely legible old script in the British Museum. Fortunately for Charles today, King Edward regarded the young Prince Edward as his favourite son and showered him with castles and land under the terms of this charter.

He was given the Cornish castles of Launceston, Liskeard, Restormel, Trematon and Tintagel and other castles in adjoining Devon, including the mighty fortress at Exeter. With the castles came the right to raise an income from all the manors, villages and farms for scores of miles around their walls.

Over the centuries most of the castles crumbled, but the estates prospered, expanding into a wide belt of rich farming country and thriving towns, stretching all the way to London.

Charles is the twenty-fourth owner of the Duchy of Cornwall. Over the years the money has flowed in but not all of the dukes had good fortune as kings-in-waiting.

Ten of them never succeeded to the throne, including young Edward, the first duke, who grew up to be the warrior called the Black Prince because of his habit of wearing black armour as he fought on numerous continental battlefields. He died before his father.

Another, Edward V, was one of the princes murdered in the Tower of London before he had a chance to sit on the throne. The Duke of Windsor, Charles' immediate predecessor, was never crowned Edward VIII; he abdicated before his coronation.

Several of them died as children before they could make use of the income or even reach the

In the country where he became a man — Australia

throne. Charles seems lucky to have survived the course so far.

The spread of the Duchy and the complexity of its affairs are enormous. Like the boss of a big business enterprise, Charles administers its affairs with the equivalent of a board of directors. To help him run what, in the 1970s, is a very up-to-date venture, there is an eight-strong Prince's Council. It includes some modern gentlemen with titles from another age, such as the Lord Warden of the Stannaries, Keeper of the Privy Seal and Keeper of the Records.

The Stannaries title comes from the Latin 'stannum' meaning tin, and goes back to the age when a large portion of income for the Duchy was from the thriving tin mines of Cornwall. The members of this group go about their work in a mansion opposite Buckingham Palace that looks as if it houses a permanent English afternoon tea-party, but on the board are some of the best financial, legal and estate management brains in the country. His financial watchdog for example, known as the Receiver General, is youthful Mr John Baring of Baring Brothers, the international merchant bankers based in the City of London.

Keeping a day-to-day watch on the assets of the dukedom is Mr Anthony Gray, who for twenty years looked after the cash for the rich Christ Church College at Oxford University. As Secretary and Keeper of the Records he is in constant communication with the Prince, advising him and receiving instructions from him, on the running of the Duchy.

Charles takes the whole business seriously, ploughing into figures, reports, plans, designs and laws on property ownership with enthusiasm. His estates are considered to be among the best run in the country.

While he was at sea he still kept an eye on what was going on ashore, an essential chore if Prince Charles Ltd was to continue as a viable proposition.

The headquarters at No. 10 Buckingham Gate is an imposing Nash-style building constructed in 1877, and houses a permanent staff of twelve altogether. Such is the size of the estate that there are five sub-offices spread throughout the West Country, including a granite, fortress-like mini-headquarters at St Mary's, one of the flowery and windswept Scilly Isles.

Mr Gray, at the London headquarters, said: 'For the past few years his naval duties prevented Prince Charles from taking a regular part in the running of the estates. His five years in the Royal Navy were followed by a busy year helping to organise the Queen's Jubilee Celebrations.

'Throughout this time though, he and I were in touch either by letter or on the telephone so he could make decisions about the Duchy. He takes a
98 detailed interest in what is happening, as you

A working day for businessman Charles in the City of London

would expect, and his concern for the well-being of the estates and those on them is immense. The Prince tries to be a good landlord and treat his tenants fairly.

'The estates are not really run as profitably as they could be. What he takes out of the Duchy is not much by today's standards, when you consider that this has got to pay for his staff at Buckingham Palace, all his living expenses and cover the many donations he makes every year to charitable organisations.

'He is hideously generous with his money and hardly ever ignores a request for help from an organisation within the Duchy. He gives away an incredible amount of his income.'

The total value of the Duchy has never been properly assessed. Because so much of it is run almost as a charitable operation, not charging really commercial rents, it only ticks over, certainly not yielding the rich pickings it would if put into the hands of hard-headed property developers.

Rents at Kennington, for example, are deliberately kept low to help the mainly elderly and poorly paid who live in the district. A visit from the landlord is not usually welcomed by most people, but when Charles visits his tenants he is greeted with bunting and cheers. They decorated the streets for him when he last wandered round his Kennington property.

Among those he met living there were his former nanny, Miss Helen Lightbody, and a dozen or more other ex-royal servants. He popped into one of the local pubs, the Sir Sydney Smith, where landlord Alfie Goff offered to pull him a pint, but Charles declined, 'I've had my fair share today, thank you.'

Charles has a home next door to the regional headquarters of the Duchy at St Mary's in the Scillies. It is on the very tip of England pointing across the Atlantic from the English Channel. The offices of the estate even have an old cannon on the lawn, put there in the sixteenth century to fight off Spanish invaders. Charles' secluded hide-away, a cottage called Tamarisk, is just a few yards along from the offices down a narrow lane. It is named after a wild shrub that grows among the rocks on the shore. When Charles flies by helicopter to St Mary's he can mix business with pleasure by relaxing in complete privacy between administering his affairs.

Tamarisk is an unostentatious three-bedroomed cottage, looking from the outside like hundreds of others on the island. It has a huge lounge, an open dining-room, a master bedroom, study, kitchen, bathroom and guest bedrooms. There is half an acre of garden, landscaped with flowers and bushes. Passers-by cannot peep in because it is surrounded by high walls.

One of the advantages of the island estate offices for Charles is that the building has extra bedrooms and flats for his friends and staff. Also, to get there, all he has to do is hop aboard a Wessex helicopter of the Queen's Flight and land on a football pitch only 300 yards away from his front door.

In accordance with the age when the title was created, Charles receives a handful of strange feudal dues, as well as cash, as master of the Duchy. Among the odd 'rents' are: a load of firewood, a grey cloak, 100 old shillings, a pound of pepper, a hunting bow, gilt spurs, a pound of herbs, a salmon spear, a pair of leather gloves and two greyhounds.

These exotic offerings were handed over to the Black Prince when he used to ride down to the West Country for drinking, wenching and hunting with his medieval friends. 600 years later the current duke is still entitled to them, though armour-clad knights no longer hammer on the doors of the poor peasantry for these gifts.

He last received such tributes in a much less rousing manner in 1973 amid the ruins of Launceston's Norman castle. Instead of frightened mobs fearful of more demands being made upon them by the royal gentry, there were thousands of happy tenants, watching a formal ceremony in which representatives of the various manors of the Duchy delivered their strange presents.

The greyhounds came from a much-decorated military gentleman, Lieutenant Colonel John Molesworthy-St Aubyn, from the splendidly named Manor of Elerky in Veryan in the West Division of the Hundred of the Powder. In return for each due the Prince handed out a white rod as a receipt. He did not hang on to the dues, however. All but the greyhounds were given to Launceston Museum; the dogs went back to their owners.

At the end of the ceremony, in the language of the Black Prince, he wished his tenants a 'peacable and quiet seizen'.

What is Charles like to work for? An easy-going and tolerant master, according to his staff.

He considers that the best training he had for running a business was in the Royal Navy, especially where man-management was concerned. His declared views on industrial relations match closely the methods he uses when dealing with his own staff and tenants.

'I think understanding on both sides is very important. I spend my life trying to understand others' problems. It is not easy, but I believe that it is most essential that one should have concern for people, help them get things off their chests.'

The businessman Prince once referred to the monarchy, jokingly, as 'one of the oldest professions in the world'. It was the late King George VI who called the Royal Family 'a firm'; Charles is proving him right in a no-nonsense, efficient way.

Chapter 8
Polo and Mozart

Ever since childhood, Charles has had a bubbling sense of humour. He says: 'The most important quality a person like myself needs is a sense of humour and the ability to laugh at oneself.'

When he was at Cambridge, he happily sat in a dustbin in a student theatre sketch about the dustman who used to wake him up every morning by noisily collecting the rubbish beneath his window. In another sketch written by himself, he came on stage underneath an umbrella and informed the audience: 'I lead a sheltered life.' For one production he volunteered to sit patiently on stage while he was bombarded with custard pies in the old Laurel and Hardy slapstick tradition.

He likes the way-out, zany variety of humour, with a bit of slapstick for good measure. His favourite comedy show was 'The Goons'. Years after this programme, which began the successful career of Peter Sellers, Charles is still a Goons addict and frequently plays their old recordings. Other comedians he likes are Tommy Cooper, Morecambe and Wise and the late Groucho Marx.

In a foreword to a book of Goon Show scripts Charles said: 'It has always been one of my profound regrets that I was not born ten years earlier than 1948, since I would then have had the pure, unbounded joy of listening avidly to the Goons each week.

'I discovered the "Ying Tong" song in record form and almost at once I knew it by heart—the only song I do know by heart. I am one of their devoted and dotty supporters.'

Royal Goon craziness livened up what was becoming a very stuffy and formal evening when Charles visited the Royal Regiment of Wales for the traditional St David's Day celebrations in the officers mess. The Prince, as their Colonel-in-Chief, called on them when they were stationed at Osnabruck in West Germany.

As a newcomer to the mess, he had to follow the custom of eating a raw leek and then bursting into song. Instead of singing something very

regimental such as 'Rule Britannia' or very Welsh, like 'Land of my Fathers', he chose the gibberish song made famous by Sellers.

Keeping a very straight face, he made the diners shake with laughter with the 'Ying Tong' song—a constant repetition of the verse: 'Ying-Tong, Ying-Tong, Ying-Tong, Ying-Tong, Tiddle-I-Po'.

'I love imitating and mimicking,' he says. 'I enjoyed acting enormously at school and university. In a strange way, so much of what one does I find requires acting ability one way or another, and I enjoy it.

'For instance, if you are making a speech it is extremely useful if you can use acting techniques; I mean timing and double entendres and everything are enormously helpful. I enjoy making people laugh if I can and I always believe humour is a very useful way of getting people to listen to what you are saying.'

His speeches show a brand of wit that clearly demonstrates the streak in him which eliminates pomposity and stuffiness about his own role in society.

Just before he took over as Captain of the *Bronington* he told a gathering of the show business fraternity—the Grand Order of the Water Rats: 'If any of you here are considering sailing on the North Seas next year, or you happen to own an oil rig in Scottish waters, I strongly advise you to increase your insurance contributions forthwith.'

He has an acute sense of the ridiculous. When he flew back from training with the Royal Marines in Canada to be invested as Great Master of the Order of the Bath, he commented to his secretary, David Checketts: 'What I find amusing is that I come back after three weeks under canvas to become the Great Master of the Order of The Bath. Rather appropriate I would say.'

Charles often turns to mimicry to amuse his friends and staff at the end of a day of being introduced to government officials or city fathers. 101

He shares with the Queen an ability to impersonate the more pompous of those he has met. A remarkable number of politicians or captains of industry would curb their tales of passing acquaintanceship with the Prince if they could see his private renderings of their behaviour.

Practical jokes are also part of his bent for comedy. At Cambridge he often introduced himself as 'Lord of the Isles' or 'Charlie Chester', justified, he thought, because he is after all Charles, Earl of Chester, and one of his ancient titles is Lord of the Isles.

He once went out to bat during a charity cricket match mounted on a pony and carrying a polo stick. When everyone was wearing name tags at a Royal Air Force dinner Charles wrote on his label: 'Watch this space.'

He pulled a fast one on a group of American photographers when he was on board the *Jupiter* and she had docked at San Diego. The pressmen were at the quayside to try to get pictures of the Prince. They asked the officer of the day to persuade Charles to come up on deck and pose for them.

The Royal Navy Lieutenant told them: 'You're wasting your time, he's very pompous and not a very likeable chap you know. He isn't very bright either, by the way. I'm quite sure he will not meet you, so you'd better go away and save your time.' The cameramen walked away grumbling without realising that they had, in fact, been talking to their prey.

Away from the responsibilities of royal duties his main hobbies and interests are wide ranging: polo, surfing, diving, flying, music, art, history, shooting, angling and archaeology.

As his experiences under the ice in Canada show, he is a highly skilled diver. He has explored old wrecks among the weeds and rocks on the bottom of numerous seas, or gone spear fishing in such exotic waters as the Pacific.

He is so keen on sub-aqua life that he always tries to squeeze a few hours of undersea exploration into a visit abroad, no matter how tight the schedule. During a tour of Fiji, for example, a well-filled diary could not stop him from venturing out with local fishermen.

Charles uses emotive prose to describe 'the supreme fascination of life below the waves'; recounting some of his adventures in the journal of the British Sub-Aqua Club, *Diver,* he mentions exploring a wreck off the British Virgin Islands and 'experiencing the extraordinary sensation of swimming inside the hull of an old schooner as if it was some vast green cathedral filled with shoals of fish.'

He once came up with pieces of eight and musket balls from a seventeenth-century wreck off the Columbian coast and plunged more than fifty feet to the muddy seabed at Spithead to look at a 400-year-old naval relic, the *Mary Rose.* One of his companions described him as 'an exceptional diver'. His taste for danger, Charles says, 'tends to make you appreciate life that much more and to really want to live it to the full.'

Polo is his one real extravagance. As he once said: 'I love the game, I love the ponies and I love the exercise. It's my favourite game.' He has played it all over the world, including India, where the game was begun and then brought to Europe by the officers of the British Raj in the nineteenth century.

Charles has been playing since he was sixteen and keeps a string of ponies at Windsor. He learned to ride ten years earlier on a small Shetland pony he used to trot gently across Windsor Great Park, where he now gallops.

He mounted up for his first chukka while he was at Gordonstoun. His father captained a team of novices, including Charles, who had the excitement of scoring a goal on his very first outing.

Although he is by nature a modest person, he succumbs to temptation now and again and puts on a bit of a show on the polo field, especially if a girlfriend is watching.

One of the regular players with Charles says: 'He is absolutely fearless. He is very aggressive and thunders along at a frightening pace. Over the past five years he has become a player of top international class.'

Another player says: 'Prince Charles is a leader with a cool head in any situation,' although someone else claims that: 'Charles shows far too much consideration for his horses and will not drive them hard enough.'

During the 1977 season his handicap was raised from two to three, an indication of his increasing prowess. In polo, unlike golf, the higher your handicap rating, the better, but Charles still has a long way to go before reaching his father's top form—eight.

Another of his greatest pleasures is to go for lonely walks over moorlands or through woods and in the Scillies he often wanders along the shoreline.

He indulges his love of an active, outdoor life by heading for the hills and grouse moors the moment the game season opens. Charles is keen on guns and his standards are as high as those of his grandfather, George VI, who was out shooting the day before he died. He is rated one of the finest shots in the royal household. He shoots at Sandringham for pheasant and partridge and in North Yorkshire and Scotland for grouse. In one noisy weekend at Sandringham Charles and Prince Philip, together with a few friends, bagged 600 birds between them.

Among his more gentle pursuits is listening to and playing music. The Prince's tastes are mainly

Charles the actor, at university, as a 'Beatle' and *(overleaf)* as a target for custard pies

classical, his favourite composers being Bach, Mozart and Berlioz. He has a passing interest in jazz but rarely bothers about pop. He used to be a fan of The Beatles though, because he thought they had an exceptional talent both as musicians and lyricists—'The more I heard of them the more I enjoyed them.'

He used to play the trumpet and the piano, but without great success. Then one evening he went to the London Festival Hall for a performance by the cellist Jacqueline Dupré and was so impressed by the rich deep sound that he decided to take up the instrument himself.

In art he prefers the paintings of the seventeenth and eighteenth centuries. He enjoys Rembrandt and Van Dyck and also Rubens and his plump ladies. He does not have much of an eye for modern artists, especially Picasso, who he regards with distaste. He is a painter of no mean skill himself. When he first tried his hand with watercolours he was taught by the notable Norfolk artist, Edward Seago.

His reading is mainly non-fiction with only the occasional novel. Generally, he tends to read history and biographies. 'When you meet as many people as I do you become curious about what makes men tick and why they tick differently,' he says. History has great significance for Charles because he is so aware of being part of the continuing story of Britain: 'I don't know whether it is me, or being born into what I was, but I *feel* history.'

This fascination for history he carried with him from Gordonstoun to Trinity College Cambridge, where he studied archaeology and anthropology during his first year.

He had an average Class II Division I pass in his tripos on these subjects before switching to modern history for his last two years at university, at the end of which he took a Bachelor of Arts Honours degree.

His mind does not lean easily towards the technology of our age, but rather towards the arts. He is particularly fond of the theatre and enjoys almost any sort of play: comedies, thrillers, musicals, or the classics such as Shakespeare and   103

(Continued on page 108)

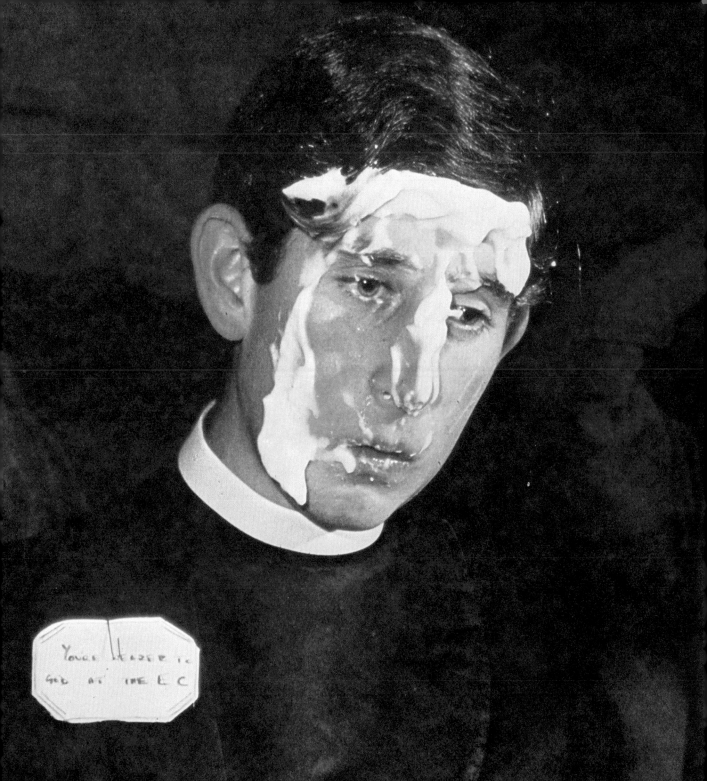

Ibsen. London, with justification, is to Charles the greatest theatrical capital in the world. Given a choice, he goes for comedies. He has to be careful whom he takes along however, because any girl he is seen with immediately becomes the subject of speculation.

He has never shown any inclination to become a leader of fashion. Sober, conventional clothes have always been his style. He seems to follow the advice given a hundred years ago by the Prince Consort to his great-great-grandfather, Edward Prince of Wales: 'A gentleman will borrow nothing from the fashion of the groom or the gamekeeper.'

He shies away from flamboyancy, prefering the discreet good taste of the well-pressed Savile Row area rather than the gaudiness and constantly changing outfits of Carnaby Street. His suits, costing £200 each, are made by Hawes and Curtis where his personal tailor is the doyen of good taste in clothes, Mr Edward Watson.

Charles orders his shirts by the dozen and ties by the half-dozen from Turnbull and Asser, the renowned blue-cottoned firm in St James's where the world's most stylish men clad themselves at nothing less than £20 a garment. Among other clients for their range of striped shirts is film star Robert Redford. The Prince's measurements, incidentally, are: chest—37 in, waist—31 in, and hips—36 in.

He had an early triumph on the fashion front at the age of five, when he was voted the 'Best Dressed Man in Europe' by the *Tailor and Cutter* magazine. He made quite a dash, in their opinion, wearing a velvet-collared coat. This award was of great assistance to the velvet industry as hundreds of thousands of mothers hurried to buy similar garments.

Later in life, however, his sartorial efforts have come under attack. The self-appointed arbiter of taste in the suiting fraternity, Mr John Taylor, said in *Style* that he thought the Prince was 'drifting into a kind of dull image of his rather circumspect father'.

Taylor went on: 'What the country needs is a Prince like one of the recent Edwards—flippant, arrogant, tasteful, stylish and full of elegance. We really do not want a royal reflection of humourless shop stewards.' As a final admonition he added:'Your average male royal looks more and more like Fred who lives on the corner.'

Anyone involved with the clothing industry has felt he has the right to take a pot-shot at the Prince. 'We want a peacock Prince,' pleaded the Tie Manufacturers Association. Become a fashion leader, a trend setter, a Beau Brummell, they said; 'Your country needs you sir.'

Tailor Watson has stood loyally by Charles. He answered the critics: 'The Prince has his own impeccable dress sense and often takes my advice on points of fashion. No amount of outside criticism would sway him to give up his own good taste in exchange for uncomfortable wear to satisfy the changing tastes of Carnaby Street.

'I've been making suits for the world's best customers for nearly fifty years and I have never come across someone as meticulous as the young Prince.'

There was hope in 1974 from across the Atlantic however. Charles was back in the best dressed list again. New York fashion expert Eleanor Lambert coupled him with 'Kojak' actor Telly Savalas as one of the international Best Dressed Men. She paid this tribute: 'For someone who is going to be a king he can be quite hep.' Eventually even the tie manufacturers relented and at the end of 1977 they nominated him the World's Best Dressed Man.

Charles had his own way of dealing with his sartorial critics when he turned up at a formal dinner of the Master Tailors Benevolent Association wearing a shabby sports jacket over his tails.

He told them: 'I am often asked whether it is because of some generic trait that I stand with my hands behind my back like my father. The answer is that we both have the same tailor. He makes the sleeves so tight that we can't get our hands in front.'

Charles is not one for discotheques, with their ear-shattering noise, smoke and shoulder-crunching crowds, although when he was in the Navy he used to go on boisterous runs ashore with his fellow officers.

In Caracas he stayed until four in the morning at a nightclub with what he described as 'a party of beautiful Venezuelan ladies', and remembers: 'When the ship sailed at 6.30 that morning I was not in a good condition at all.'

A perfect evening for him is to take a pretty girl to the theatre followed by a quiet supper either at Buckingham Palace or in the corner of a discreet restaurant. He likes parties but does not drink much. He always says that he can get 'drunk' on atmosphere alone. At a party he tries to make everyone relaxed, put them at ease and make them accept him as just one of the gang.

He has a few close friends who he trusts completely, certain that they will not let him down by spreading gossip about him or telling any tales about his behaviour when he lets his hair down in private. Despite these friends, he leads a fairly solitary existence—'In a sense I am alone, and the older I get the more alone I become.'

At Buckingham Palace Charles lives in a three-bedroomed flatlet cut off from the rest of the building on the second floor. It is decorated in pale colours and furnished in a leathery masculine style.

The bookshelves contain mainly volumes on

Swapping experiences with surfers at Coolangatta, New South Wales

history, archaeology and art. Other shelves have his collection of Eskimo soap carvings including one of a huge musk-ox, and still others hold eighteenth-century objets d'art bought with the help of a friend who searches around the London salesrooms for him. The Prince is fussy about keeping the place neat and tidy and apt to get annoyed over clutter.

When he has the opportunity of an evening alone in his rooms at the palace, he likes to watch comedy shows and documentaries on television or read about archaeology.

His new home, Chevening House near Sevenoaks, in the stylish stock-broker belt of Kent, is a tranquil retreat away from the bustle of London, a place where Charles will be able to relax in idyllic secluded grounds. There are 3,000 acres of park and woodland, twenty-four acres of landscaped gardens and a four-acre lake.

Chevening was for 250 years the home of the Earls Stanhope, a family that for seven generations devoted itself to public service, composed of politicians, soldiers, inventors and generous donors to charities. When the seventh

earl died without an heir it was stated in his will that the fine old house and grounds should be given to the nation. He hoped Charles would take up the offer and continue to care for the family seat.

The late earl had arranged an endowment of £250,000 before his death in 1967 for the maintenance of the house. By the time Charles accepted the place this money had increased to nearly a million pounds, all of which was put aside to restore the building to its former glory. A place fit for a Prince and, eventually, his family to live in.

Charles' living quarters are in the centre block. On the ground floor there are three main reception rooms, a small sitting room and a kitchen. The first floor has four bedrooms, a bathroom and a dressing room. The second floor has six bedrooms, two dressing rooms, four bathrooms and a kitchenette.

As part of the conversion and renovation work Charles had loud-speakers fitted in all the living rooms and his bedroom . . . so he can have music wherever he goes.

109

DAMN IT, I TOLD YOU NOT TO RIDE HIM SO HARD.

HE'S YOUR HORSE, YOU RIDE HIM.

Charles on leave from *HMS Jupiter,* telling a sailor's tale to his cousin, the Duchess of Kent

Some of Charles' happiest moments are when he is with his family, a close-knit group whose sense of unity provides a welcome relief from the pressures around it. They value and protect one another.

When Charles is abroad he is in constant touch with his mother and father, brothers and sister or grandmother and aunt, either by telephone or by letter. No member of this group does anything without discussing it first with the others and hardly any commitment is made without family approval.

The Queen, who succeeded to the throne when Charles was three years and three months old, had also been brought up in a warm family circle. The Victorian habit of banning the children to the nursery and rarely seeing them until they could either shoot or ride, had long since died by the time of her own childhood. Because of the loving atmosphere she remembered with her parents, she arranged that there would be no barriers of governesses and nannies between herself and her own children.

Now that Charles is older and Princess Anne has a family life of her own, the Queen sees less of her eldest children though the Prince tries to be with his mother and father as often as he can. Every morning when he is in London he begins his day by leaving his own rooms at the front of Buckingham Palace to join his parents for breakfast in their quarters at the rear of the building.

His mother's day usually starts at eight o'clock in the morning, listening to the radio, and reading the morning papers and personal letters. Breakfast is at nine o'clock with Prince Philip and the rest of the family. In the palace grounds below the window, a bagpiper plays a few cheerful tunes to get the morning moving.

Until lunchtime the Queen concentrates on reading State papers, dealing with official correspondence, and discussing the running of the household with her staff. She holds audiences at noon and after a light lunch she leaves for afternoon engagements. At five o'clock in the afternoon she feeds her corgis—distributing the food into several bowls with a silver fork and spoon. If neither she nor Philip have any evening

engagements they often eat a simple supper on a tray, watching television comedy shows.

The Queen and Prince Charles have much in common. He takes after her in his kindness and gentle qualities. She does not like change and Charles has the same conservative attitude. They are both aware of the continuing constitutional roles they shoulder. They sense that they not only belong to the nation and Commonwealth but are also the ongoing link of this heritage.

In childhood Charles was somewhat shy and introverted, in contrast to Anne, who was ebullient and outward going. As a toddler he would snuggle up beside his mother on a settee and look quietly at a picture book, or listen to her as she read him a story. The most popular ones were the tales of Beatrix Potter and the adventures of Baba the Elephant and Tin-Tin.

He had enough boyish spirit in him however for the Queen, just like any other mother, to have to cope with the pranks and mischief of her son. He raced round the corridors of Buckingham Palace with his friends, played risky games of hide-and-seek on the roof of Windsor Castle, or slipped pieces of ice down the collar of a footman. When he deserved it he would get a good spanking, particularly if he was caught being rude to the servants. The Queen took a very stern view of this.

Her Majesty also taught him the value of

money, restricting his pocket money to the equivalent of twelve pence a week until he was ten years old, when he was given a rise which made it twenty-five pence. As part of the training for a ceremonial life, Charles and Anne were taught to stand motionless for long periods, to accustom them to the duties ahead.

Hundreds of requests came for the young Prince to make public appearances but the Queen resisted them all, no matter how worthy the cause. She remembered how, as a young princess in the war years, she was suddenly thrust into the public arena and she insisted that her son should first of all have a normal childhood, as far as this could be arranged. So the Queen protected Charles and brought him up carefully to the stage when he was gradually made aware of his state duties.

Her Majesty was also determined that her son 113

would not become a palace wastrel, a mere understudy, deprived of any responsibility and forever waiting in the wings. She had seen too much of this in the history of her family. Charles was to be made aware of his future role at the right time, then be prepared for it and given something worthwhile to do in the meantime.

The Queen took special care over the education of the Prince. Sending Charles away to school, rather than having the traditional private tuition for him, was to set a royal precedent. She decided that, unlike his predecessors, he should go out and meet his future subjects. Her Majesty had been educated behind the railings of Buckingham Palace by a succession of governesses and tutors. Charles was given the chance to go beyond the royal stockade, and live among ordinary people.

She helped her son through all the usual growing pains of youth and his moments of bewilderment at life. Her encouragement was always there whenever he thought the going was too tough. When he first went away to school she wrote to him almost daily, feeding him family gossip to keep up his spirits. At university Charles occasionally found the task a struggle and felt lonely. The Queen would visit him privately in his rooms at Trinity College, where they would talk over his problems while he fried a simple meal for the two of them.

The Queen attended to her son's upbringing with a typical mother's gentleness but Prince Philip provided a grittier influence.

With the family at Badminton Horse Trials. *Left to right:* Viscount Linley, Prince Philip, Prince Andrew, Princess Margaret

George V once said: 'My father was frightened of his father . . . I was frightened of my father . . . and I'm going to see to it that my children are frightened of me.'

Royal paternal attitudes have changed considerably since the beginning of this century, when that Palace edict was issued. Charles and Philip have a very close relationship, based not on fear, but on love and respect for each other's achievements.

Their personalities differ considerably. Prince Philip has always been the more abrasive while Charles has more gentleness of spirit. One of the Duke's friends once said: 'Charles is not a bit like him.'

At first Charles seemed to try hard to emulate

his father. He was tempted to adopt Philip's occasionally high-handed style. But as he grew out of his teens the Prince developed a likeable personality of his own, while his father began to mellow.

They tend to have the same mannerisms: the brisk walk, the habit of clenching their hands behind their backs, and tossing their heads when laughing; Charles too walks around with his left hand thrust casually into his jacket pocket. He has inherited his father's sense of humour; both like zany, outrageous slapstick rather than sharpness of wit.

Otherwise their tastes are usually quite different. Charles adores music for instance, whereas Prince Philip finds it agonizing to have to sit through a concert. The young Prince can enjoy solitary pastimes, while the Duke is much more gregarious.

Some people close to the family think Princess Anne takes more after her father than does her elder brother.

When Charles was a child, Prince Philip did not see much sign of the eventual virile young man in his son. But his father was determined that his son would not have a pampered life. When Charles was a schoolboy, Philip once noticed a servant hurrying to close a door that his son had failed to shut. He shouted: 'Leave it alone, man. He's got hands. He can go back and do it himself.'

Prince Philip wanted him out of the palace and into the world, rubbing up against other children ,seeing how others lived. He said: 'We want him to go to school with other boys of his generation and to learn to live with other children. To absorb from his childhood the discipline imposed by education with others.'

He also wanted Charles to pick up a few bruises and get used to the hard knocks of tough physical activities. Dancing lessons were stopped, music lessons cut down and instead, Charles was sent off to the playing field in Chelsea to get into the rough and tumble of soccer with other youngsters. He also went to a private gymnasium twice a week for gymnastic work-outs.

Prince Philip took him out in bitter wintry weather to teach him to shoot in the mud and puddles of marshes and over the heather around Balmoral, where Charles shot his first grouse when he was ten years old. He taught him how to fish. Philip is now less keen on fishing than Charles, who finds the Queen Mother a more amenable riverside companion.

When Philip was at home he would spend an hour after tea teaching his son to swim in the pool at Buckingham Palace. Charles took to the water without a hint of nervousness and could swim a length before he was five years old. Father and son would have a boisterous game of football in the palace grounds, with the corgis barking round 115 their heels. Now and again the Queen and toddler Anne might join in the fun.

Nearly all his physical skills were taught to Charles by his father. In this way they grew closer to each other, and Philip was delighted to see his son developing into a more self-confident youngster.

But Charles has never had the Duke's ambition to excel at organised games. He still shows little enthusiasm for team games, such as rugby, soccer and cricket. Individual achievement, where he is testing himself rather than others, has been his forte, hence the generally solitary pursuits he tends to go in for . . . diving, surfing, flying. His only concession to 'team spirit' is polo, which has four men on each side.

Philip introduced Charles to sailing, but he did not develop the same passion for it as his father. The Duke and he rarely go sailing together these days because they do not seem to see eye-to-eye when they are in a boat. Charles explains frankly: 'I remember one disastrous day when we were racing and my father was, as usual, shouting. We wound the winch harder and the sail split in half with a sickening crack. Father was not pleased. Not long after that I was banned from the boat after an incident cruising off Scotland. There was no wind and I was amusing myself taking pot-shots at beer cans floating around the boat. The only gust of the day blew the jib in front of my rifle just as I fired. I wasn't invited back on board.'

The Duke, in consultation with the Queen and her advisors, also influenced the choice of schools for their offspring. He had his way first over the preparatory school Charles went to before moving on to public school. Philip attended Cheam School, which is set in sixty-five acres of grounds on the Berkshire border. It has a history of teaching the aristocracy and the sons of the rich going back as far as the early seventeenth century. Charles, too, was sent there.

The really decisive part played by the royal father in helping to bring out latent manly qualities in Charles was when the time came to select a senior school for him at the age of fourteen.

Eton, the traditional establishment for top young English gentlemen, was, at first, favoured by the Queen. Charles' name had been put down for a place when he was born. Philip had other ideas. He wanted—and got—his other alma-mater: tough, authoritarian Gordonstoun set on a bleak stretch of Scotland's west coast in Morayshire and based on the principals of German refugee educationalist Dr Kurt Hahn.

Gordonstoun had been good enough for the Duke. He thought its harsh, cold-shower regime had done him a world of good, so why should it not do the same for his eldest son? At the time,

even Dr Hahn had his doubts. Charles gave no sign at that age of ever becoming a chip off the old block. Philip persuaded the Queen however, that Gordonstoun would bring Charles out and make him more self-assertive. In short, toughen him up and smarten him up.

When the young Prince went to the grim institution he was still shy and withdrawn. Charles remembers now that all the tales he had heard about it made the school seem 'pretty gruesome'. It was a very nervous young man who was flown by his father up to Morayshire to spend a few bracing years there and, hopefully, end up a man. Philip had reminded him 'not to let the side down'.

The place was mainly a collection of crude huts. His dormitory had unpainted wooden walls, bare floors and uncomfortable iron beds. There was the obligatory cold shower to be taken every morning, no matter what the weather. As the school is situated in one of the more exposed and rugged parts of Scotland, the temperature was usually at shivering level. Even the school motto—'Plus est en vous' (There is more in you)—typified a harsh system aimed at stretching to the full both physical and intellectual capabilities.

To bring him down to earth and away from any fancy ideas he might have of being a special sort of fellow from the land of palaces, his housemaster gave Charles a particularly humiliating daily task in his first term—emptying the dustbins. Dr Hahn described the place and his methods as one where 'the sons of the powerful can be emancipated from the prison of privilege.'

Charles may have been reluctant to be submitted to the rigours of Gordonstoun, but he never quarrelled with his father's decision. He hated the school at first, became terribly homesick and did not fit easily into the regime. After four years Charles ended up liking the place, just as his father had done. He became head boy and, shrugging his shoulders, pointed out that it was not really as tough as he had expected it to be.

He excelled in geography and modern languages, captained the school's cricket and hockey teams and represented Gordonstoun in inter-school athletics meetings. He also took the title role in a production of *Macbeth*.

A few years after leaving Gordonstoun though, he said: 'I did not enjoy school as much as I might have, but that was because I am happier at home than anywhere else.'

Charles once spoke of his father's influence on his education: 'His attitude was very simple. He told me the pros and cons. Out of all the possibilities and attractions he told me what he thought best. Because I had come to see how wise he was, by the time I had to be educated I had perfect confidence in my father's judgement. When children are young you have to decide for them. How can they decide for themselves?'

Schooldays over, Charles became much more of the man Philip had been seeking. They built up an adult affinity that is just as strong today. It was his father's influence above all others, that persuaded Charles to choose a career in the Royal Navy. Philip felt that Charles should have some sort of Service career. When his son was eighteen, the Duke said: 'It would seem both natural and needful for him to have some Service experience. I think that having a longish period in one Service, or attachments to all three, will be very useful to him in later life.'

The best training, so far as Prince Philip was concerned, was in his own beloved Navy. His reasons: 'It has several advantages as a training ground. You learn to live with people of all sorts. You have to develop a professional ability. Going to sea is not merely a military operation, it is a professional one as well—getting a ship from one place to another. Altogether you live in a highly technological atmosphere—probably a good introduction to the kind of thing which controls our whole existence.'

So Charles took his father's advice and joined the Navy. It must have been one of the proudest moments in Prince Philip's life when he was piped aboard his son's command, the *Bronington*, in the spring of 1976.

He joined skipper Charles at Rosyth, the Scottish naval base where he had served as a sub-lieutenant during the Second World War. On this occasion he wore the gold-ringed uniform of an Admiral of the Fleet.

A smile from father to son as they saluted each other put over clearly the 'well done' message.

One great passion father and son have in common is polo. Philip took up the game shortly after his marriage so that he could share the Queen's enthusiasm for horses. As a toddler Charles would watch the Duke play and throughout his early teens was constantly pestering his father to let him mount up and join him. The Prince used to help around the stables or act as a sort of 'squire', handling the polo sticks or standing ready with a bottle of water between chukkas.

Philip thought he was too young to take part in the game until he was in his mid-teens, but until then he taught him how to handle a pony and the difficult knack of ball control. The pair of them would ride off into Windsor Great Park for practice sessions, which came in useful during Charles' later playing.

He and Charles both love flying. Philip has clocked up several thousand hours as a pilot all over the world. He has flown almost every type of aircraft, from helicopter to sea-plane and even transatlantic airliners. With his skills in a cockpit

Three young royals on duty in New Zealand

he not only encouraged Charles' flying instincts but gave him helpful advice.

When Charles received his pilot's wings at Cranwell, the Duke was so cock-a-hoop with pride that he told photographers; 'I'll stand on my head if you want me to.'

Philip shares with Charles an interest in preserving the environment. He has noticed how the Prince has got involved in the Welsh countryside: 'I think he has really got a very genuine affection for and interest in Wales; largely because if your name is attached to a place you automatically feel that you belong to it.'

It is through his father that Charles keeps in   117

touch with his continental relations: the royal houses in Norway, Denmark and Sweden and the German branches of his lineage. Both the Queen and Prince Philip have scores of German relatives as a result of the marriage of Queen Victoria to Prince Albert. In addition, three of Philip's sisters married German princes.

In some quarters of Britain, hostility towards our former enemies still, sadly, lingers on. Because of this, the Queen cannot be seen to have too much to do with the German branches of her family, but there seems to be little objection to Philip and Charles flying over to spend a few days with kinsmen in the odd Bavarian schloss.

Anne has always been more assertive than Charles, with less tolerance of other people. She has a no-nonsense attitude to life that puts her in line with her father. From childhood on though, when Anne used to try to boss Charles, they have had great affection for each other. Neither of them take any major step without discussing it together. Over the years they have built up great confidence in the other's judgement.

Another member of the family with whom Charles has tremendous affinity is Princess Margaret: 'Aunt Marg' or 'Charley's Aunt' as she has called herself. She helped to introduce him to music by giving him impromptu piano lessons or by amusing him with her skill at improvising light-hearted tunes. He and Margaret also have a love for the theatre and both of them are frustrated actors.

The Queen Mother has a very soft spot for Charles, who greatly reminds her of her late husband, King George VI, to whom she was so deeply attached. She sees something of the late King's sensitivity to other people's thoughts and feelings in him. A great bond has developed between them. When Charles travels, he sends a steady stream of letters to 'grannie', sharing his experiences with her.

During the Australian period of his education, when he was beginning to get homesick, she flew out to join him for a few days. They went fishing for trout in the Snowy Mountains. At Balmoral they often go off casting for salmon together in the wild waters of the river Dee.

Balmoral, the Royal Family's Highland estate, was Charles' favourite childhood home and he still likes to spend his holidays there. The way of life is more informal and the only faces around are those of old friends.

For about six weeks each summer the Prince is able to lead a normal life with his family in the friendly seclusion of Balmoral. Here he goes fishing or sets off alone for walks across the heather. It's a place where Charles can enjoy his favourite role in life . . . the eldest son with his family.

119

The new generation — Andrew, Mark and Charles

Chapter 10
King in Waiting

When Charles was about to graduate from Cambridge, he was given a booklet called *Choosing a Career.* His fellow students may have found it useful, but he had no need of it.

The Prince's future has never been in doubt, and he has been prepared for his destiny. He is almost ready to be a king, and more than competent to cope with the responsibilities of monarchy.

He has gone through the traditional training of an heir apparent—a short career in one of the Services—and is now taking a bigger part in official life. The lack of a bride seems the last barrier to his final readiness for the throne.

The King-to-be has been carefully groomed for the part, but unlike an actor, he does not know when he will have to go on stage to play the role. The date of the 'opening night' is still unknown. There has been much speculation though, about the possibility of the Queen abdicating early, to make way for Prince Charles while he is still young.

The throne did not come to Queen Victoria's eldest son, Edward Prince of Wales, until he was

sixty. He became bored with waiting and turned to a dissolute life among shady friends and mistresses. Whilst Charles does not show any of the basic character defects of Edward VII, it would be a pity, some argue, if he had to hang around too long before his coronation.

The Queen happily is still a healthy woman, happy with her job, and as deeply interested as ever in the affairs of State. The constant travel and public engagements of the Silver Jubilee celebrations proved arduous for her occasionally, but that was an exceptional year.

Charles has dismissed suggestions that his mother should soon give up the throne in his favour. He sees no reason why she should retire. He feels that, because of the vast constitutional and political knowledge a monarch acquires by the time he or she reaches normal retirement age, the sovereign is then at a 'most useful stage'.

If the Queen lives to the ages of her mother, grandmother, or great-great-grandmother Queen Victoria—eighty-two—it could be the beginning of the twenty-first century before Charles reaches the throne. No wonder he has forecast that it might be as long as forty years before he is crowned, though one does not know how seriously he takes this proposition.

A youthful king would be popular both at home and abroad. The Queen was only twenty-six when she came to the throne and there were hopes of a new expanding Elizabethan Age for Britain. For many reasons that feeling of a national renaissance slowly died away amid a shattered economy and disintegrating colonial outposts. Could a young leader like Charles, with his tremendous energy, put vitality and purpose back into the country again? Rekindle the spirit that his mother generated in her day? Provide a new unifying force for the Commonwealth?

Unlike the profligate Edward VII, Charles has had the opportunity to be trained for all the duties of kingship, and every chance to partake in royal affairs. He does not feel the frustrations that drove Edward into the life of a playboy.

While waiting, Charles feels that he can still contribute something useful to the life of the monarchy and the country, such as the work he did towards the organising of Jubilee Year, or his active interest in young people's problems and the efforts he makes on behalf of Wales.

Since leaving the Royal Navy Charles has taken the trouble to study in greater detail the constitutional role of the Crown, though he believes real knowledge of what a king can and cannot do comes from experience. 'You learn the way a monkey learns, watching its parents,' he once told *The Observer*.

He has been trained for kingship in a period when society has become more egalitarian. We are now in the age of the common man. During the

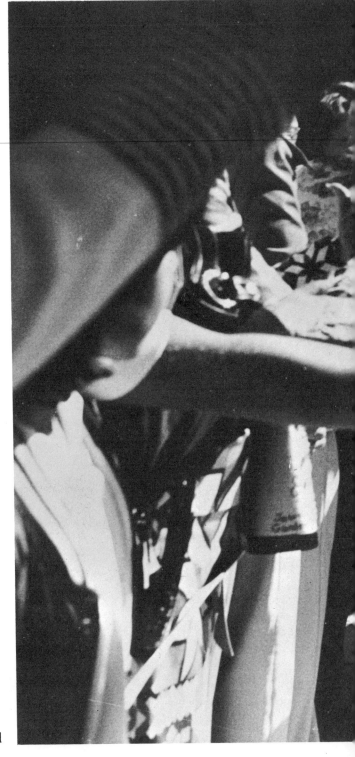

Queen's reign the social order has been changing at an increasingly accelerated pace, a phenomenon that the Queen and her advisors have taken into account in the training of Prince Charles. As a result he has a much greater affinity with student protestors, trade unionists, or the sons of dustmen for example, than his predecessors had.

The monarchy has kept in step with the developments in the streets outside its palaces and castles. Charles revealed his awareness of the new society when he said: 'In these times the monarchy is called into question—it is not taken for granted

Above: Charles' bodyguards watch closely as he is mobbed by fans in Texas; *Previous page:* Charles with Farah Fawcett-Majors in Hollywood

as it used to be. In that sense one has to be far more professional I think, than one ever used to be.'

He feels that the palace is keeping pace with the times, and the Royal Family is changing its life-style. Pointing this out, when addressing the New South Wales Parliament in Sydney, he remarked that it was not always easy to do this: 'It is more difficult to adapt when the accepted patterns of life and society change so unusually fast.' He thought however, that because the monarchy was adapting to new conditions, the

institution had become one of the strongest supports of a stable government in Britain.

This change in royal life-style began for Charles, one could say, with the circumstances of his birth. He was the first heir to the throne for centuries to be born without the mother suffering the embarrassment of having an obligatory Minister in the room. This custom was intended to ensure that a child was truly of the royal line and not a waif smuggled in by means of the bed-warmer.

When Queen Victoria gave birth to the future

Edward VII, the Minister present said to her: 'Congratulations, Your Majesty, you have a wonderful boy.' Victoria, imperious as ever, even in those circumstances, retorted from the bed: 'Prince you mean, Minister—Prince!'

When the Prince takes his throne it will more than likely be as King Charles III, but if he wishes he could choose another name. A monarch is not restricted to the names with which he was baptised. Even if he sticks to his four Christian names he could also be known as King Philip, King Arthur or King George VII.

Whatever kingly name he picks it is to be hoped that he fares better than the previous rulers named Charles. Charles I was beheaded in front of the Banqueting Hall in Whitehall one winter's day in 1649, while Charles II, the pleasure-loving 'Merry Monarch', is reputed to have died from mercury poisoning 1685. He had a fatal tendency to meddle in the wonders of chemistry.

The line of succession to the throne after Charles is: Prince Andrew, Prince Edward, Princess Anne and her offspring, Princess Margaret, Viscount Linley, Lady Sarah Armstrong-Jones, The Duke of Gloucester, Prince William of Gloucester, Prince Richard of Gloucester, The Duke of Kent, the Earl of St Andrews, Lady Helen Windsor, James Ogilvy, Miss Marina Ogilvy, The Earl of Harewood, Viscount Lascelles and the Hon. James Lascelles.

Discovery of his fate came to Charles when he was about eight years old 'in the most ghastly inexorable sense'. He remembers: 'I didn't suddenly wake up in my pram one day and say "Yippee". I think it just dawns on you slowly, that people are interested in you and you slowly get the idea that you have a certain duty and responsibility. I think it's better that way, rather than someone suddenly telling you.' He knows he is one of a dying breed, representing an institution constantly under attack, and that he will be king of a country that has known better days. He has great faith in Britain, however, and an unfashionable belief in what the country still stands for.

He said after one trip to Canada: 'I've been all over the world and I always feel how marvellous it is to come back to Britain. You can read the papers when you're abroad and you think everything is coming to an end. But you discover that things are going on the same as always and you feel happy to be back.

'These things that are so important we take for granted . . . our traditions and our institutions. This long tradition of basic freedom, which in so many cases, doesn't exist in other countries. We need to be reminded of these very important essential freedoms, which matter more than any others, make Britain what it is to us and also make Britain what it is to other people. All over the world people look to Britain for an example and a 125

With the stars of M.A.S.H. comedy series
(Picture: Bob Millenara)

lead in so many different ways.'

Rapid social changes trouble him. 'I rather think that things are tending to change too quickly. People have not had time to catch up psychologically with the rate of change. I think this poses problems of all sorts. People don't really know where they stand. They don't know what's going to happen next and they can't plan for the future. They can't look ahead. I think that rapid change is something I find difficult to keep up with.'

Yet he is optimistic about succeeding in his changing world: 'I'm one of these people who believe strongly that one should adapt to changes, particularly in my position. The one thing you cannot afford to do is to get left miles behind.

'Likewise, you don't want to be too far ahead. I think you always want to be just a little bit behind, but adapting gently and slowly. In some cases taking the initiative and doing something before it's forced on you.

'I do worry about the future, but I think if one can preserve one's sense of humour, ability to adapt and perhaps help to calm things down and to provide a steadying influence, all will be well.'

Whatever he does before his coronation, he is a well-equipped heir. No king in British history has made so great an effort to get to know so many of his future subjects, to learn so much about the countries he will rule and explore so many different parts of the world.

Prince Charles happily combines an insatiable curiosity about people with great personal charm. He seems to have met everyone from cannibals to astronauts, from charladies to film stars and his easy manner has made friends of them all.

During his tour of America towards the end of Jubilee Year he could be seen cracking jokes and holding his own in the razzmatazz of some of Hollywood's big names; he even managed to steal the limelight from superstar Farah Fawcett-Majors of TV series 'Charlie's Angels' fame, when he met her and her husband, Lee Majors — the six-million-dollar 'bionic man'. Charles also enjoyed a trip round the film studios, indulging his curiosity and his love of comedy by watching the shooting of the 'M.A.S.H.' series.

The ordinary citizens of San Francisco were as impressed as the film stars with Prince Charles' ready smile and friendly quips, when he took a ride on one of their famous cable cars; earlier on that trip, visiting San Antonio in Texas, he was besieged by a crowd of admirers who almost pulled him off his feet in their enthusiasm.

Texas provided another exciting experience when he tried his hand at cattle-driving on the ranch of Mrs Anne Armstrong, the former United States ambassador in London. He really saw some action when, with the guidance of Mrs Armstrong's husband Tobin, he was shown how to rope and herd several hundred steers.

Visiting Hollywood and Texas, Alaska and New Guinea is the glamorous, fun side of Charles' job, but the other, more serious aspects of his future are always at the back of his mind and for him they are just as exciting.

Of the task ahead, he once said: 'I've been trained to do it and I feel part of the job. I have this feeling of duty towards England, towards the United Kingdom and the Commonwealth. I feel there is a great deal I can do if I am given the chance to do it.'

In the next few years he may join the Diplomatic Service, perhaps doing a job linked with exporting British goods. He is also tipped as a Governor General of Australia, a place he is very fond of and where most people think the world of him. He is one of the few acceptable 'Poms' to a nation that is becoming disenchanted with Britain. He could heal this rift.

He regards the year he spent at school in Australia as 'the most wonderful period' in his life. The Australians responded to his affection for their country and themselves with such endearing terms as: 'Good on yer, Pommy bastard'. Part of his transition from nervous teenager to confident man took place there; away from the protecting arms of his family he learned to stand alone.

It was Australia that opened his eyes—'You are judged there on how people see you and feel about you. There are no assumptions. Having a title and being a member of the upper classes, as often as not militates against you. In Australia you certainly have to fend for yourself.' He grew to love the rough-tongued, tell-it-to-yer-straight Aussie character. He liked the muscular and dynamic life.

An appointment as Governor General could happen after his marriage and would give him and his wife two or three years of running a 'junior court' before returning to Britain, and a possible coronation.

Charles' secretary, Squadron Leader Checketts, who has been close to the Prince for ten years, has said of him: 'He's living as part of the modern scene, creating his own niche in it.

'He's still a very sensitive person with a tremendous warmth of human sympathy. He's concerned about lots of things, particularly about young people. He doesn't care too much about himself. He's both interested and interesting.

'We're jolly lucky having this combination of characteristics in the person who one day, no doubt, will be our next king.'

Once in Ottawa the Prince said of being a king: 'It's a fascinating job and I'm looking forward to the future.'

So far he has shown he has the courage to tackle anything that comes his way. He seems unlikely to falter in the years ahead.